eat.shop nyc 2nd edition

an encapsulated view of the most interesting, inspired and authentic
locally owned eating and shopping establishments in
manhattan, brooklyn, queens and the bronx

**researched, photographed and written by kaie wellman, anna h. blessing,
camas davis, jan faust dane and jon hart**

cabazon books : 2010

table of contents

notes on nyc

W: If there was a reality show called *Survivor: Big City*, I have no doubt that New York City would be victorious. Since its founding as New Amsterdam in 1624 and forty years later becoming New York City, the big island (Manhattan) and its four sibling boroughs (Bronx, Queens, Brooklyn and Staten Island), have withstood some tough times—from the battles of the American Revolution to being on the verge of bankruptcy in the '70s to 9/11 and now the Great Recession. But this tenacious city has battled back like Omarosa, righteously keeping its mantle as the most exciting, vibrant city this side of Mars.

When we began work in the fall of 2009 on this new edition, the *eat.shop* crew knew we would be facing a formidable task. The small local eating and shopping establishments of this city had been hit hard. A number of great places that had been featured in the first edition of *eat.shop nyc* and the precursor to that, *eat.shop brooklyn*, had closed their doors. So when Anna H. Blessing, Jan Faust Dane, Jon Hart and Tamas Davis (who makes her *eat.shop* debut on this title) and I hit the streets, we went looking for good news. And we found a lot of it. After criscrossing the city from north to south, east to west, we chose 127 amazing small, locally owned businesses that were flourishing.

I can't say enough about these businesses. Some have been around for almost a hundred years, some have been open two months. Some are high-end, some won't cost you more than an Alexander Hamilton to enjoy. While many are embracing an early 1900s aesthetic, others are looking towards the future. What they all have in common is that they embrace the "keep on, keepin' on" spirit, and are doing it with aplomb.

Though this book is all about the local eating and shopping experience, we can offer up some suggestions for other activities around the city. Here you go:

> *On the Water*: NYC and Brooklyn are basically islands. Paddle around Brooklyn in a rented kayak or canoe launched from Red Hook piers, or adventure straight through Brooklyn on the Gowanus Canal. For less work, and more play, hop into a water taxi and tell them you want a true round trip ride.

> *The High Line*: The most highly anticipated "park" to open in NYC since Central Park opened in 1859. Running from Gansevoort Street in the Meatpacking District up through Chelsea, this is a great place to take a breather and take in the view across the Hudson.

> *Red Hook Ball Fields*: Okay, this involves eating. But the fields were closing for the season when we were in production on this book. From mid-April through October this is the place to come on the weekends for great Latino food. Head to Clinton Street, corner of Bay.

> *The Museums*: This is the motherlode of museums, and you can't visit here without spending time some. Google museums of New York City, and Wikipedia has a good list. Some of our faves? Moma, American Museum of Natural History, PS1, Cooper-Hewitt and Museum of Sex, to name a few.

about eat.shop

• All of the businesses featured in this book are locally owned. In deciding which businesses to feature, that's our number one criteria. Then we look for businesses that strike us as utterly authentic and uniquely conceived, whether they be new or old, chic or funky. And if you were wondering, businesses don't pay to be featured—that's not our style.

• A note about our maps. They are stylized, meaning they don't show every street. If you'd like a more detailed map (and you really need one for this city), pick up a Streetwise map for NYC or we have an online map with the indicators of the businesses noted > map.eatshopguides.com/nyc2. And a little note about exploring this city. Subways will get you just about anywhere you need to go (except Red Hook), and they are almost alway quicker. Also great in NYC are the buses. There's no better way of getting the lay of the land by hopping on a bus. Get an unlimited ride metro card in any subway station kiosk (available in 1, 7, 14 and 30 days) and use it for both the subway and the buses. For Red Hook, take any train to Jay Street / Borough Hall or the M / N / R to Court Street. Then catch the B61 bus.

• Make sure to double check the hours of the business before you go as they often change seasonally. Also, the pictures and descriptions for each business are meant to give you the feel for a place. Don't be upset with the business if what you see or read is no longer available.

• Small local businesses have always had to work that much harder to keep their heads above water. During these rough economic times, some will close. Does this mean the book is no longer valid? Absolutely not. You can go to the *eat.shop* website to the NYC page to see which businesses have closed.

• The *eat.shop* clan consists of a small crew of creative types who travel extensively and have dedicated themselves to great eating and interesting shopping around the world. Each of these people writes, photographs and researches his or her own books, and though they sometimes do not live in the city of the book they author, they draw from a vast network of local sources to deepen the well of information used to create the guides.

• Please support the indie bookstores in New York City. To find these bookstores, use this great source. www.indiebound.org/indie-store-finder. We also support the *3/50 project* (www.the350project.net) and in honor of it have begun our own challenge (please see the back inside cover of this book).

• Though all of the other *eat.shop* titles retail for $14.95 and are 192 pages, *eat.shop nyc* is like many things are in this city: bigger. This book features 127 businesses and is 284 pages, therefore it's a bit more expensive: $16.95.

• There are three ranges of prices noted for restaurants, $ = cheap, $$ = medium, $$$ = expensive

• Authors are noted as such: Kaie Wellman (creator and publisher of the series) > KW, Anna H. Blessing > AB, Jan Faust Dane > JFD, Camas Davis > CD and Jon Hart > JH.

previous edition businesses

if you own the prevous edition of *eat.shop nyc* (or *eat.shop brooklyn*), make sure to keep it. Think of each edition as part of an overall volume of books, as many of the businesses noted below are just as fantastic as the day they opened.

at

bistro
l di là
ma
ngel's share
arney greengrass
ohemian hall
eer garden
ierkraft
rown café
andle 79
asellula
ha an
hip shop
hoice market
anal
'amico foods
iner
ressler
umont
gg
isenberg's
et sau
or de mayo
ankie's 457 sputino
anny's
eemans
randaisy bakery
abana outpost
i
laboratorio del gelato
ckson diner
e & pat's
eens steakhouse
efi
yotofu

la luncheonette
locanda vini e olii
marlow & sons
mary's fish camp
mas (farmhouse)
moto
myers of keswick
odessa
one girl cookies
otafuku
pasita
pies n thighs
pop burger
poseidon greek bakery
province chinese canteen
(now mantao chinese
sandwichs)
prune
roasting plant coffee co.
roomali
rosenthal wine merchant
sahadi's
sal's pizzeria
saxelby cheesemongers
sfoglia
shanghai cafe*
staubitz market
steve's authentic
key lime pie
taim falafel & smoothie bar
the good fork
the greene grape
the little owl
the spotted pig
tia pol
tony & tiny's pizza

shop

a detacher
allan & suzi
alpana bawa
amarcord
annelore
bblessing
bird
bonnie slotnick
cookbooks
brooklyn general barber
bu and the duck
castor & pollux
cb i hate perfume
city joinery
cog & pearl
cozbi
d / l cerney
darr
de vera
e. vogel
elizabeth street gallery
freemans sporting club
golden calf
grdn
global table
halcyon the shop
hats. by bunn.
in god we trust
j. leon lascof & son
jutta neumann
kid o
layla
lord willy's
loveday 31
lyell

mantiques modern
matter
maxilla and mandible
mick margo
mini jake
mini mini market
moon river chattel
n harlem boutique
nydesignroom
oak
odin (pas de deux)
ps9
purl / purl patchwork
roberta freymann
roberta roller rabbit
secondhand rose
stewart / stand
subdivision
the future perfect
the paris apartment
tinsel trading company
wonk
woodley & bunny
yoya / yoyamart

if a previous edition business does not appear on this list, it is either featured again in this edition, as closed or no longer meets our criteria or standards.

where to lay your weary head

there are many great places to stay in new york city, but here are a few of our picks:

the ace hotel
20 west 29th street (murray hill)
212.679.2222 / acehotel.com
standard double from $150 restaurant: the breslin
notes: west coast utilitarian chic comes east

the jane hotel
113 jane street (west village)
212.924.6700 / thejanenyc.com
captain cabin (w/bath) from $225 standard cabin (shared bath) from $89 restaurant: cafe gitane
notes: tiny rooms, groovy vibe, easy on the pocketbook

the standard
848 washington street (meatpacking district)
212.645.4646 / standardhotels.com
standard double from $335 restaurants & bars: the standard grill, the boom boom room, biergarten
notes: outstanding modern architecture straddling the high line

hotel aka
four locations: central park, times square, sutton place and united nations
hotelaka.com
one bedroom suites from $400
notes: gorgeous, spacious apartment like suites

the chelsea hotel
222 west 23rd street (chelsea)
212.243.3700 / hotelchelsea.com
standard double with kitchenette from $200
notes: legendary funky hotel that puts the "e" in eccentric

the nu hotel
85 smith street (park slope)
718.852-8585 / nuhotelbrooklyn.com
standard double from $200
notes: one of the only boutique hotels in brooklyn

and a couple more: hotel east houston: affordable hotel in the les (hoteleasthouston.com), thompson hotels: five properties, mainly downtown, for the chic nyc experience (thompsonhotels.com), w hotels: four locations with union square a favorite (starwoodhotels.com/whotels), doubletree metropolitan: midtown convenience, huge rooms, super affordable (metropolitanhotelnyc.com) and homeandaway.com, check out property 232515 in hell's kitchen and710guestsuites.com, chic apartment rentals in harlem.

2nd avenue deli

my favorite jewish deli ever

162 east 33rd street. between lexington and third. 5 / 6: third avenue
212.689.9000 www.2ndavedeli.com
mon - thu, sun 6a - midnight fri - sat 6a - 4a

opened in 1957. owners: the lebewohl family
$-$$: all major credit cards accepted
breakfast. lunch. dinner. first come, first served

murray hill / gramercy park > **e01**

KW: Never in the history of doing these books have I ever had as much fun as I had eating lunch at *2nd Avenue Deli*. From the moment I walked in here, Mo and Karen and Steve took me under their wing. Soon I was sitting at the counter with a big bowl of matzoh ball soup kvetching away with my countermates Morton and Jordi. Plates and plates of food kept appearing before me like I had a Jewish fairy grandmother whipping things up in the kitchen. I truly died and went to kosher deli heaven. By the time I left, hours later, hugs were in order. I love this place.

imbibe / devour:
dr. brown's cel-ray soda
bosco & soda
chopped liver
matzoh ball soup
meat & potato knish
hot pastrami sandwich
gefilte fish
rugalach

abraço

espresso counter with exceptional small plates

86 east seventh street. between first and second
4 / 6: astor place > l: 1st avenue > r / w: eighth street
www.abraconyc.com
tue - sat 8a - 4p sun 9a - 4p

opened in 2007. owner: jamie scott mccormick owner / chef: elizabeth quijada
$: cash only
coffee / tea. lunch. treats. first come, first served

east village >

JFD: With a hearty, "What you need, brotha?" Jamie, the magnetic owner and coffee puller of *Abraço* greets his customers. Chances are, if you go to this small espresso counter, you are seriously in need of one of Jamie's skillfully made, perfectly balanced coffee drinks. What you might not have realized, until you bite into one, is that you also needed chef / partner Elizabeth's dense, flavor-rich olive cake. And now, I'm telling you, brothas and sistas, that what you really really need is to check in here daily. Once will do, but twice is better.

imbibe / devour:
individually dripped coffee
café cortado
roasted vegetable with cheddar fritatta
sunchoke ricotta & mint sandwich
olive oil cake
pistachio cookie
pomegranate chocolate cake with almonds
pain perdu

arthur avenue

the best little italy in new york city

2327 - 2350 arthur avenue. between fordham and 183rd
2: 180th street (then take the bx12 bus westbound)
www.arthuravenuebronx.com
seven days a week

businesses began opening in the early 1900s
$-$$: all major credit cards accepted
breakfast. lunch. dinner. grocery. first come, first served

belmont >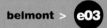

KW: It's no big secret that Manhattan's Little Italy is a shadow of its former self. When you walk around what used to be a vibrant neighborhood, the feeling is more LittleItalyland, then anything authentic. Most New Yorkers agree that to get a truer experience, you need to head to the Belmont neighborhood in the Bronx, to *Arthur Avenue*. Yes, it's a long subway ride plus a bus ride, but don't wimp out as this is a worthy experience. Pick up a ring of lard bread at *Madonia Brothers*, some sweet sopresate from *Calabria* and then have lunch at *Roberto's* or *Dominicks*. Ahh, this is *la dolce vita*.

imbibe / devour:
my favorite arthur avenue businesses:
  randazzo's seafood
  calabria pork store
  madonia brothers bakery
  borgatti's ravioli & egg noodles
  arthur avenue cigars
  teitel brothers
  dominick's of arthur avenue

barbarini

alimentari, mercato and ristorante

225 front street. between beekman and peck slip
2 / 3 / 4 / 5 / j / z / m: fulton street > a / c: broadway-nassau
212.227.8890 www.barbarinimercato.com
mon - sat 10a - 10:30p sun 11a - 9:30p

opened in 2009. owners: claudio marini and stefano barbagallo
$$: all major credit cards accepted
lunch. dinner. brunch. wine / beer. grocery. reservations accepted

financial district > **e04**

CD: Italian men in leather coats will no doubt be sipping espresso outside of this very Italian mercato and alimentari. And inside *Barbarini*, you will find rows of pasta and canned tomatoes, and a glass case bursting with sopresate and salami. Also gelati. Check. Olive oil and mostardo. Yes. Just about anything you can imagine in an Italian larder is sold here. You can also take a seat in the light-strewn back dining room and have the cooks make you something delicious like spaghetti with sicilian tuna and capers. This place has authentic appeal, with the perfect touch of slickness on the finish.

imbibe / devour:
aranciata
espresso
speck, taleggio & frisee sandwich
ham & shredded eggs sandwich
grilled shrimp & avocado salad
scaloppina di pollo al vino bianco
lasagna pasticiata alla bolognese
a scoop of gelato

bark hot dogs

haute dogs

474 bergen street. corner of flatbush. 2 / 3: bergen street
718.789.1939 www.barkhotdogs.com tw: @barkhotdogs
mon - thu 11a - midnight fri 11a - 2a sat 9a - 2a sun 9a - 10p

opened in 2009. owners: brandon gillis and joshua sharkey
$: visa. mc
breakfast. lunch. dinner. beer / wine. first come, first served

park slope >  **e05**

JH: We drive gasoline-powered cars because Henry Ford started us down that road a long time ago. And we eat boiled-to-oblivion, mystery-meat hot dogs because that's what we've become accustomed to. However, there is a new dog in town. *Bark Hot Dogs* elevates the lowly hot dog to a show dog. Top-notch ingredients and condiments are used, often citing where they were sourced. The hot dogs themselves snap with freshness and flavor, and you know right away that this dog does not have a first name spelled O.S.C.A.R. Hurray for innovation! Think of them as the Prius of hot dogs.

imbibe / devour:
six point brownstone ale
peanut butter shake
beans & frank dog
pickle dog
slaw dog
onion rings
salt & pepper fries
cookie whoopie pies

beer table

artisan beers and snacks

427b seventh avenue. between 14th and 15th. f: seventh avenue
718.965.1196 www.beertable.com tw: @beertable
daily 5p - 1a

opened in 2008. owner / chef: justin philips
$$: all major credit cards accepted
dinner. snacks. first come, first served

park slope >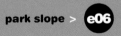

JH: I've heard lardo, absinthe and small batch vodka all proclaimed as the 'next big (foodie) thing,' to which my jaded mind thinks 'well, they're over.' Even though a lardo sandwich sounds worthy of angina, I prefer the classics. And it doesn't get more classic than beer. Or does it? At *Beer Table,* knowledge and conviction supplant hype with truly inspired nightly selections of esoteric beers. Justin expertly talked me through the list of taps, and I decided on a Piet-Agoras. It was hoppy and smooth, complex and unlike anything I've tasted before. I was hooked. Who needs hype when you've got the goods?

imbibe / devour:
piet-agoras
hik blond
fentimans ginger beer
birra del borgo 25 dodici
ricotta with olive oil & bread
pickled eggs with jalepeño powder
schlenkerla pork sausage with salt potatoes
il laboratorio del gelato

birdbath bakery

neighborhood green bakery

145 seventh avenue south. corner of charles. a / b / c / d / e / f / v: west fourth
646.722.6570 www.birdbathbakery.com tw: @birdbathbakery
mon - fri 8a - 8p sat - sun 9a - 8p

opened in 2007. owner / baker: maury rubin
$-$$: all major credit cards accepted
breakfast. lunch. treats. first come, first served

west village >

JFD: As predictable as swallows to Capistrano, I return to *Birdbath Bakery* whenever I come to town. My powerful homing instincts tell me that here, in this little nest of a bakery, I'll find refuge from the bustling streets outside. More importantly, I'll find the sustenance required to power any other flights around the city I might have planned. I can't help but sing loudly the praises of their giant cookies, buttery pastries and inventive sandwiches. And no worries about a Silent Spring on account of *Birdbath*; the bakery employs truly green and sustainable practices. Make sure it's on your migratory path.

imbibe / devour:
farmer's lemonade
ronnybrook farm milks
pretzel croissant
housemade granola
blueberry honey scone
leek, scallion & mint pizza
smoked tofu & japanese hummus sandwich
coconut cookie

bklyn larder

glorious prepared foods, cheeses and groceries
228 flatbush avenue. between bergen and sixth. 2 / 3: bergen street
718.783.1250 www.bklynlarder.com
mon - sat 10a - 9p sun 10a - 8p

opened in 2009. owner: francine stephens owner / chef: andrew feinberg
$$: all major credit cards accepted
lunch. dinner. treats. grocery. first come, first served

park slope > 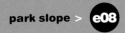 **e08**

JH: As a kid, I would walk through our local Piggly Wiggly humming Peggy Lee's "Is That All There Is?" OK, I was a weird kid, but even at age 12 I knew there was potential for more in terms of groceries and food shopping. My tune changed recently. Literally a dream come true, *Bklyn Larder*, sells top-notch, hand-chosen staples in the most beautiful environment. If the meats, cheeses or gelati aren't made in house, then you best believe they are the best on the market. I'm older now but still singing Peggy's tunes. *Bklyn Larder*, you give me a "Fever."

imbibe / devour:
larder made:
  fresh pancetta
  porchetta
  rabbit rillettes
  hams
squid salad
homemade almond butter
roasted chickens

blaue gans

a nyc wirtshaus

139 duane street. between church and west broadway. 1 / 2 / 3: chambers street
212.571.8880 www.kg-ny.com tw: @blauegans
see website for hours

opened in 2005. owner / chef: kurt gutenbrunner
$$-$$$: all major credit cards accepted
lunch. dinner. brunch. reservations recommended

tribeca >

KW: There are people who believe the only reason to eat is to fuel the body. Though I'm sure these folks have an enviously low body fat ratio, they are missing out on one of life's great pleasures: eating really good food. If you embrace self-depravation, you might miss out on Kurt Gutenbrunner's mini-Austrian empire in NYC which includes the fine dining mecca *Wallsye*, *Café Sabarsky* (see page 31), *The Upholstery Store* and *Blaue Gans*, my favorite. This spot is a Bavarian-style gastropub where the neighborhood gathers to eat hearty, delicious fare. Health food it's not; happy food—absolutely.

imbibe / devour:
07 gruner veltliner marc aurel caruntum
kônig pilsner
apfelschnapps
market bean salad with pistachios & sour cream
smoked trout palatschinken, baby beets,
   horseradish & ligonberries
weibwurst & brezel
apple strudel with toasted almond ice cream

botanica

fresh cocktails

220 conover street. corner of coffey. bus: 61 / 77
718.797.2297
tue - thu 6p - midnight fri 6p - close sat 10a - 3a sun 10a - midnight

opened in 2009. owner: daniel preston
$$: all major credit cards accepted
dinner. brunch. full bar. first come, first served

red hook > **e10**

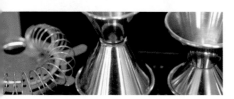

CD: I've always assumed that the no booze before noon rule only applies to those who refuse a well-rounded breakfast with their cocktail. But if I am going to eat a big breakfast for the sake of alcohol, my accompanying cocktail better be just as well-rounded. Which is why *Botanica* is the bar for me. When I walked in for Sunday brunch, the room was light filled and airy, and the fresh-squeezed Bloody Mary was—without any doubt—the best I'd had. As was the Blackberry Daiquiri and the Hemingway. If I lived in Red Hook, I'm pretty sure my mornings would never get off the ground.

imbibe / devour:
fresh-squeezed bloody mary
pink slipper
blackberry daiquiri
the hemingway
strawberry basil martini
free-range poached eggs, bacon & tomato
anchovy crostini with white bean & basil
goats milk ice cream & strawberry basalmic

brooklyn flea

flea market food booths and much, much more

sat: 176 lafayette avenue. between vanderbilt and clermont
sun: 1 hanson place. corner of flatbush
www.brooklynflea.com tw: @bkflea
sat - sun 10a - 5p all trains: atlantic avenue / pacific street
(check website for seasonal location changes)

opened in 2007. owners: eric demby and jonathan butler
$-$$: mainly cash
lunch. treats. first come, first served

fort greene > e11

CD: It was a simple smear of handmade ricotta that convinced Kaie and me to include *Brooklyn Flea* in this book. Part antique showcase, part outdoor gallery for local artisans, and part food mecca, *Brooklyn Flea* looks and functions like a regular open air flea market, but it's the local cheese and chocolate makers, the taco slingers and pickle masters that really lend it cache. That ricotta? It was puffy and light, spread on a piece of bread, topped with arugula and prosciutto. After eating our way through the aisles, it was clear: this is where food-obsessed Brooklynites go to get sated.

imbibe / devour / covet:
salvatore ricotta, arugula & prosciutto bruschetta
mcclure's pickles
fine & raw chocolates
liddabit brittle
the good fork dumplings
the good batch stroopwafels
blue canary vintage
charlie's fortune telling at anodyne

café sabarsky

elegant spot for a viennese lunch and pastries

1048 fifth avenue. corner of 86th. 4 / 5 / 6: 86th street
212.288.0665 www.cafesabarsky.com
mon 9a - 6p wed 9a - 6p thu - sun 9a - 9p

opened in 2001. owner / chef: kurt gutenbrunner
$$-$$$: all major credit cards accepted
breakfast. lunch. dinner. coffee / tea. first come, first served

upper east side > **e12**

JH: The reason to put up with sky-high rents and rat-filled subways in New York, in my humble opinion, is the proximity to grandeur. Why do you think Grand Central Station got its name? Because it's not in Peoria. Another example of grand elegance in this city is lunch at *Café Sabarsky*. Attached to the Neue Gallery of Art in a former Vanderbilt mansion, it can't help but give you a "I'm not in Kansas anymore" reaction. Whether it is the walnut-paneled room or the proximity to priceless Schieles, it makes the whipped cream that much richer and the klimttorte that much more decadent.

imbibe / devour:
06 sauvignon blanc steinmühle
kaiser mélange
celery root salad with apples & walnuts
speck with melon & mustard-pickles
chestnut soup with armagnac prunes
hungarian beef goulash with quark späetzle
liverwurst with onion confit sandwich
klimttorte mit schlag

cho dang gol

delicious korean cuisine

55 west 35th street. between fifth and sixth. b / d / f / n / q / v / r / w: 34th street
212.695.8222 www.chodanggolny.com
mon - sat 11:30a - 10:30p

opened in 1997. owner / chef: kim bong ok
$$: visa. mc
lunch. dinner. beer / wine. reservations recommended

midtown westside > e13

JH: The difference between freshly made tofu and the stuff you buy at D'Agostino's is huge. Akin to the difference between a Swanson's steak dinner and going to *Peter Luger*. *Cho Dang Gol* looks like hundreds of other places along 35th street in Koreatown—but it has one silky, pillow-y advantage; they make their own tofu here. That makes it worth visiting for that alone as it's heavenly delicate. But the rest of the offerings are very good too. Classic stone bowl bibimbap is better than any I have had—it's a far cry from Hungry Man.

imbibe / devour:
baek se ju (korean herbal wine)
ob korean beer
spicy kimchi pancake
tofu trio
handmade tofu
classic stone bowl bibimbap
mountain bowl
fresh leek pancake

classic coffee shop

a slice of the real new york city
56 hester street. corner of ludlow. f: east broadway
917.685.3306
mon - fri 8a - 4p

opened in 1976. owner: carmine morales
$: cash only
breakfast. lunch. first come, first served

chinatown >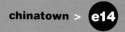

KW: If you are going to spend any time in this city, there are certain food items that are imperative to the NYC experience. A bubbling hot slice of white pizza. A skyscraper of a pastrami sandwich. And the breakfast of choice for hordes of on-the-run New Yorkers: an egg sandwich. There are a number of ways to order this, but my favorite is a mini omelette tucked inside a buttered roll. Add a dash of salt and pepper. Devour. If you are downtown, grab one at *Classic Coffee Shop*. This tiny neighborhood diner is a slice of old New York, which makes it a breath of fresh air.

imbibe / devour:
classic egg cream
little hug juice
coffee, white
egg sandwich on a roll
grilled cheese sandwich
sardines sandwich
ruffles
wrigley's gum

di fara pizza

legendary brooklyn pizza

1424 avenue j. corner of 15th. q: avenue j
718.258.1367 www.difara.com tw: @difaras
wed - sun noon - 4:30p, 6 - 9p

opened in 1964. owner / chef: domenico demarco
$-$$: cash only
lunch. dinner. first come, first served

midwood >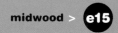

CD: When Domenico pulls a pizza from the ancient oven at *Di Fara*, he often uses his bare hands to do so. His gnarled and floured digits are those of a true master—one who's been stretching dough, grating mozzarella and snipping fresh basil since 1964. If there's any music playing here it's classical, but often it's silent, and everyone standing in line whispers as if at church waiting for the sermon to begin. Indeed, we are all here to worship at *Di Fara's* altar. And when we finally take that first bite of salty, cheesy, tangy, crunchy perfection, a communal murmur can be heard: yes, there is a God after all.

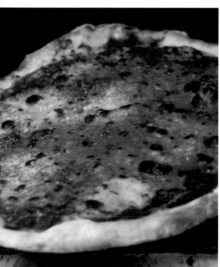

imbibe / devour:
coca cola
ginger ale
pizza:
  plain pie
  square pie
  artichoke pie
  special pie
cheese & prosciutto calzone

dirt candy

extravagant vegetarian fare

430 east ninth sreet. between first and a. l: first avenue > 6: astor place
212.228.7732 www.dirtcandynyc.com tw: @dirtcandys
tue - sat 5:30 - 11p

opened in 2008. owner / chef: amanda cohen
$$: all major credit cards accepted
dinner. wine / beer. reservations recommended

east village > **e16**

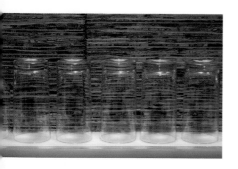

JFD: I admit, like many conscious eaters of this era, I'm sometimes a bit tortured by my feelings about meat. I can go on about this at length, but "boorrrriiinngg," I hear Amanda, the owner/chef of *Dirt Candy,* interrupt in my head. She'll tell you, in her tartly hilarious blog, that she's not interested in your health or your politics. What she enjoys are vegetables, and she has found some innovative ways to cook them. And while a few of the dishes bear the sometimes perverse (and entertaining) hallmarks of molecular gastronomy, others are simply prepared vegetables that just taste really good.

imbibe / devour:
08 michel torino don david torrontes reserve
intelligentsia coffee
jalapeño hush puppies with maple butter
kimchi donuts
stone-ground grits
asparagus paella
golden beet pappardelle
popcorn pudding

double crown

the flavors of the british empire in southeast asia
316 bowery. corner of bleecker. 6: bleecker street
212.254.0350 www.doublecrown-nyc.com
see website for hours

opened in 2008. owner: avroko executive chef: brad farmerie
chef de cuisine: christopher rendell
$$: all major credit cards accepted
lunch. dinner. brunch. afternoon tea. full bar. reservations recommended

east village >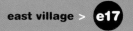

KW: During a typical NYC weekend, the streets of the city are flooded with locals, bridge and tunnelers, and tourists. To walk on Broadway in Soho requires a stealth ability to dodge the masses armed with their bulging shopping bags. Suggestions for a calmer weekend experience? Head east for afternoon tea at *Double Crown*. This lushly designed ode to British colonialism in India and Singapore is the perfect spot to settle in. The tea set is piled high, and the tea—if you so choose—can be boozy. And when the night comes, head through the concealed doorway to *Madam Genevra* to continue the relaxation.

imbibe / devour:
strawberry & basil boozy tea
cucumber & black peppermint boozy tea
sweet lemongrass tea
devonshire tea:
  coconut labne
  piccalilli
  coronation chicken
  scone

dovetail

humble three-star restaurant

103 west 77th street. between columbus and amsterdam
1: 79th street > b / c: 81st street
212.362.3800 www.dovetailnyc.com
see website for hours

opened in 2008. owner / chef: john fraser
$$$: all major credit cards accepted
lunch. dinner. brunch. full bar. reservations recommended

upper west side > e18

CD: It's hard to believe that any neighborhood in this vibrant city could be considered the veritable equivalent of milquetoast, but the Upper West Side has this reputation, especially when it comes to dining. That is, until *Dovetail* showed up on the scene with John's playful new American cuisine. Though the décor is a bit bland, the menu is full of bright spots. A chestnut soup sprinkled with pumpernickel croutons, currants and garnished with a luxurious foie gras cream? Yes. Kumamoto oysters suspended in cucumber sauce with American caviar? No milquetoast here.

imbibe / devour:
d'groni cocktail
amontillado "napoleon" sherry bodegas hidalgo
lamb's tongue muffaletta presse, olives, capers
halibut confit, cabbage, quail egg, truffles
hudson valley baby pig, apples, celery, lentils
grilled matsutake, braised chicken, sunchokes
chamomile panna cotta
vermont vs. the old world cheese plate

dutch kills

working man's cocktail bar

27-24 jackson avenue. between dutch kills and queens
n / w / z / 7: queensboro plaza
718.383.2724 www.dutchkillsbar.com
mon - sun 5p - 2a

opened in 2009. owners: richard boccato and sasha petraske
$: cash only
full bar. first come, first served

long island city > e19

CD: If I were a piano tuner at the Steinway factory in Long Island City, I'd go to *Dutch Kills* for an old-fashioned after work. If I were a stevedore working on the docks, I'd buy my happy hour beer here. If I were a post-apocalyptic performance artist who just installed my video art at PS1 down the street, I'd come for an 1887 Manhattan to celebrate. And if I looked like Tom Waits, I'd bring my guitar, play it in the back, tap my cigarette ashes on the sawdust floor and blend into the darkness. But while this is undoubtedly an everyman's bar, the cocktails are far from everyday. In fact, they transcend.

imbibe:
bartender's choice
chin chin
st. charles punch
1887 manhattan
archangel
gershwin
water lily
queens park swizzle

el quinto pino

bar de tapas

401 west 24th street. corner of ninth. e: 23rd avenue
212.206.6900 www.elquintopinonyc.com
sun - thu 5p - midnight fri - sat 5p - 1a

opened in 2007. owner / chefs: alex raij and mani dawes
$-$$: all major credit cards accepted
dinner. full bar. first come, first served

chelsea >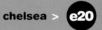

KW: Last year Jan and I spent a riveting day together at the Book Expo in Javits Center. We spent hours fending off folk who came to the event to "shop," i.e., get free swag by swiping any items that weren't nailed down. By quitting time, we were zonkered. To revive, we headed for *Tia Pol* (featured in the first edition) and their stellar tapas. It was instant resuscitation. So when it came time to do this book, and I had a long day scouring the city, I aimed for *Tia Pol's and Txito's* (see page 125) offspring, *El Quinto Pinto*. This eensy tapas spot is perfect for after-work drinks and nibbles. Say ahhhhhh.

imbibe / devour:
granizados horchata
juve y camps rosado
estrella damm beer
torreznos
gambas al ajillo
saldaditos de pavia
uni panini
pringá

flushing, queens dumpling crawl

search for the ultimate chinese dumplings

s & t: 39-07 prince street 718.359.1601 zjgt: 40-52 main street 718.353.6265
xa: 41-28 main street (shi hong mall) cknd: 133-31 39th avenue (flushing mall)
7: flushing main street

$: varied payment options
breakfast. lunch. dinner. first come, first served

flushing >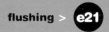

	HONG BONG STYLE RICE CAKE	炒米粉 STIR-FRIED RICE NOODLE	$1.25
4PCS)	蜜棗粽子 SWEET RICE CAKE	$1.75/個(EACH)	
		酸辣湯 HOT & SOUR SOUP	$2.5 $1.5
ACH)	茶葉蛋 TEA EGG	$1.00/3個(3PCS)	
		綠豆湯 GREEN BEAN SOUP	$1.2
ACH)	甜豆漿 SWEET SOYBEAN MILK	$1.50(大)(L) $0.75(小)(S)	
		銀耳湯 TREMELLA SOUP	$1.7
ACH)	咸豆漿 SALTY SOYBEAN MILK	$2.25(大)(L) $1.25(小)(S)	
		冷凍湯包 FROZEN SMALL BUN	$11.
ACH)	甜豆花 SWEET SOYBEAN CURDS	$2.50(大)(L) $1.50(小)(S)	
		各種冷凍水餃 ALL KINDS FROZEN DUMPLINGS	$11

JH: Ah ha! An *eat.shop* loophole! I came to Flushing with its amazing Chinatown to find the place with the best dumplings. This proved to be a hard job as deciding between plump and meaty versus tender and delicate—or steamed rather than fried—sent me into a panic. Each dumpling I ate only further whet my appetite making me want to continue my greedy search. Narrowing down to one favorite place seemed impossible. Then a carb-induced moment of inspiration happened. I decided to list all of my favorite spots and call this spread a dumpling crawl. Which was all I could do when I was done.

imbibe / devour:
my favorite spots:
  spicy & tasty
  zhu ji guo tie
  xi'an famous foods
  chinese korean noodles & dumplings

49

fort defiance

a great spot to get happily sated

365 van brunt street. between dikeman and coffey. bus: 61 / 77
347.453.6672 www.fortdefiancebrooklyn.com tw: @fortdefiance
see website for hours

opened in 2009. owner: st. john frizell
$: cash only
breakfast. lunch. dinner. brunch. full bar. first come, first served

red hook > e22

CD: On the wide spectrum of modern-day cocktail connoisseurs, I'm somewhere in the middle. I'll geek out about bitters and gins and jiggers with the best of them, but in the end I believe a drink is a drink—it should have a few solid ingredients in it and be poured with care by a well-versed bartender. And I like to drink surrounded by happily sated folk. No other bar cum café cum restaurant personifies this philosophy better than *Fort Defiance*, where owner and expert hooch slinger St. John pours some of the best drinks around and always keeps it just this (right) side of real.

imbibe / devour:
vesper cocktail
journalist cocktail
muffaletta
deviled eggs
rabbit stroganoff
big braised pork shank
pimento cheese with ritz crackers
meatloaf sandwich

gottino

enoteca e salumeria

52 greenwich avenue. between sixth and seventh. 1 / 2 / 3: 14th street
212.633.2590 www.ilovegottino.com tw: @ilovegottino
mon - fri 8a - 2a sat - sun 11a - 2a

opened in 2007. owner / chef: jody williams
$$: all major credit cards accepted
breakfast. lunch. dinner. first come, first served

west village > e23

AB: If I wasn't addicted to good food before, eating at *Gottino* solidified my position as a diehard lover of all things edible. I should clarify though. If food looks and tastes like cardboard and glue, then (obviously) I couldn't care less about it. But when food is both delicious and beautiful to look at, as it is at *Gottino*, I am 100% committed. At this place even a simple piece of toast is transformed into a piece of edible art. As for saying anything else here with words, I'm going to hold off and let the pictures do the talking.

imbibe / devour:
04 canneto vino nobile
07 ribolla gialla petrucco
stracchino crostini
carciofi e mentuccia crostini
shaved brussels sprouts with pecorino
olive oil whipped house cured salt cod
braised rabbit pot pie
nutella & toast

hallo berlin

german soul food cart

54th street at fifth avenue, north side
v: 5th avenue-53rd street > f: 57th street > n / r / w: 60th street
212.333.2372 www.halloberlinrestaurant.com (see website for other locations)
mon - fri 11:30a - 3:30p

opened in 1981. owner: rolf babiel
$: cash only
lunch. first come, first served

midtown westside > e24

JFD: Puns abound when a cart sells German sausages. The best is "New York's Wurst Pushcart." At *Hallo Berlin*, the puns are put aside for nicknames like the Volkswagen, the BMW or the Mercedes. And while puns and cute names are fun, at the end of the day, a cart doesn't win a Vendy Award for Best Street Food unless it's putting out a killer product, which this place does. The days I was there, sleeting rain pelted a dozen people who stood patiently to receive their uber-delicious dog. I admire their perseverance but hope they don't visit daily, or else they'll be saying, "Hallo, cardiologist!"

imbibe / devour:
pepsi
clausthaler na beer
berliner curry wurst
bavarian meatballs on bun
alpenwurst
schnitzel sandwich
german fries
imported gurke

N "SOUL" FOOD COMBO MIXES

RMAN FRIES - RED & WINE CABBAGE - SAUTEED ONION - CRUSTY ROLI

UL FOOD MIX	ONE CHOICE OF ANY WURST	6 00
NUL FOOD MIX	NO CHOICE - COMES WITH BRATWURST&BERLIN FRANK	8 00
EAL	ANY KIND OF WURST, SAUTEED ONION, POTATO SALAD, BAVARIAN MEATBALL	7 50
ENUE COMBINATION	TWO CHOICES OF ANY WURST 1-8	10 00
UL FOOD MIX	COMES WITH A BMW - MERCEDES - PORSCHE	11 00
DIET PLATE -LOW CARBOHYDRATE	ONE VEAL, PORK & BEEFWURST,	11 00

henry public

eats and drinks with speak-easy ambiance
329 henry street. between atlantic and pacific. 2 / 3 / 4: borough hall
718.852.8630 www.henrypublic.com
mon - thu 5p - 2a fri 5p - 4a sat noon - 4a sun noon - 2a

opened in 2009. owners: matt dawson, jen albano, tracy meyer and jeremy dawson
$$: cash only
dinner. full bar. first come, first served

cobble hill > **e25**

JH: When times are flush in NYC, wallet-busting restaurants are all the rage. But when times are challenging, places start to harken back to the last great depression. A perfect example is *Henry Public*. Think of a Dixie-esque speakeasy serving killer cocktails and hearty burgers. Opened by the folks behind the popular *Brooklyn Social*, this crew knows how to create a place that's 100% authentic and full of vitality. With glimmers of hope on the economic horizon, 14k-gold-dusted sweetbreads will surely return. But *Henry Public* will continue to thrive. A happy upside to the economic downturn.

imbibe / devour:
kings county sour cocktail
two-cents fancy cocktail
marrow bones with toast
grilled cheese with apple slices
lettuce & watercress salad
juniper pickles
turkey leg sandwich
new york egg cream

57

home/made

down-home wine bar

293 van brunt. between pioneer and king. bus: 61 / 77
347.223.4135 www.homemadebklyn.com
see website for hours

opened in 2009. owner / chef: monica byrne owner: leisah swenson
$-$$: cash only
brunch. dinner. wine / beer. first come, first served

red hook >

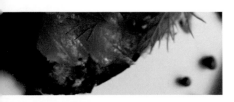

CD: Some years ago, when I lived in Brooklyn, my boyfriend and I considered it a vacation to drive to Red Hook and spend the afternoon wandering the 'hood's scrubby streets and deserted docks. Back then there was nothing much to see, save for a few renegade art installations and an old coffee shop. Today, however, Van Brunt is lined with spots including *Home/Made*, a tiny eatery that feels more like a shabby chic living room than a restaurant. And when you're seated on one of the overstuffed couches, a glass of wine in hand, a savory tart on the way, the grubby urban frontier outside seems far away.

imbibe / devour:
brooklyn oenology "motley cru"
brundlmayer sekt brut
robert sinskey vin gris pinot noir
open-face smoked salmon with chevre
warm potatoes provençal
parmigiano stuffed dates wrapped in bacon
blt with roasted red pepper aioli
charcuterie plate with cornichons

i sodi

authentic italian

105 christopher street. between bleecker and hudson. 1: christopher street
212.414.5774 www.isodinyc.com
daily 5:30 - 11p

opened in 2007. owner / chef: rita sodi
$$-$$$: all major credit cards accepted
dinner. reservations recommended

greenwich village >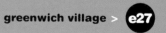

AB: Some people are hard-wired to dig deeper and work harder and because of this, their creative output outshines almost everybody else's. Rita is one of these types, and people flock to her eponymous restaurant, *I Sodi*, like it's the North Star. From the olive oil she hand presses from the trees on her property in Tuscany to the fresh pasta she rolls out daily—it is clear that this is a person who truly cares about the food she serves to her devoted and hungry followers. I can say that the lasagne I had here was the best I've ever eaten, and I will beat a path to *I Sodi's* door every chance I get.

imbibe / devour:
negroni
pasta & ceci minestre
lasagne ai carciofi
lasagne al sugo di carne
tortelli burro & salvia
galletto schiacciato
branzino alla griglia con fagioli
risotto cacio & pepe

james

old-world euro meets seasonal american

605 carlton avenue. corner of st. marks. q / b: seventh avenue > 3: bergen street
718.942.4255 www.jamesrestaurant.com
dinner nightly 5:30 - 11p sun brunch 11a - 3:30p

opened in 2008. owner / chef: bryan calvert owner: deborah williamson
$$-$$$: all major credit cards accepted
brunch. dinner. full bar. first come, first served

prospect heights > e28

JFD: It's very in the mode these days to name an establishment after a grandparent. If a place annoys you, then this seems like a saccharine act. But if you really like a spot, then you'll embrace the sentimentality. The latter describes how I feel about *James*, named after the grandfather of chef Bryan. I don't know if the eponymous James actually cooked this way—I know my grandparents boiled hot dogs, kept frozen Velveeta around and drank grapefruit juice out of a can—but that's why it's Bryan's restaurant and not mine. Sentimentality aside, the food here is what will make a memory.

imbibe / devour:
goose island oatmeal stout
st. anne's cocktail with st. germaine & basil
cauliflower soup with smoked sturgeon
rock shrimp risotto with lemon tomato jus
sautéed skate with "la ratte" potatoes
ricotta pancakes with stone fruit syrup
lavender crème brûlée with fresh berry salad
grilled lemon pound cake with figs in port wine

joseph leonard

crushable american "brasserie" cuisine

170 waverly place. corner of grove. 1: christopher street
646.429.8383 www.josephleonard.com
see website for hours

opened in 2009. owner: gabriel stulman chef: jim mcduffee
$$-$$$: all major credit cards accepted
lunch. dinner. brunch. full bar. first come, first served

greenwich village >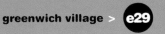

AB: In every book that I've authored for this series, there's always one place that I can't get out of my mind. *Joseph Leonard* is this place in this book. I liken my experience here to a really great first date. At the initial meeting, I felt pure (okay, it was lustful) attraction. As the date progressed, I relaxed and was soon besotted by the utterly warm, yet non-smarmy charm of my companion. By the end of the date I was absolutely sure that *Joseph Leonard* was "the one." Now my only worry is how many other people have also fallen for *Joseph* as I don't know if I can share.

imbibe / devour:
rye tea cocktail
professor bucky
frisee & lardon
warm bean salad
pastrami sandwich
roast chicken for two
jonah crab claws
warm brownie

kalustyan's

spice heaven

123 lexington avenue. between 28th and 29th. 6: 28th street
212.685.3451 www.kalustyans.com
mon - sat 10a - 8p sun 11a - 7p

opened in 1944
$-$$: all major credit cards accepted
light meals. grocery. first come, first served

murray hill / gramercy park > **e30**

KW: For some, traveling overseas means visiting famous landmarks and taking pictures of said places and picking up a couple of souvenirs. When I travel abroad, I tend to steer clear of famous spots, I take pictures of things like dried leaves and I fill up my suitcase with local foodstuffs and everyday items like toothpaste. Instead of flying half way around the world, I could also stock up at *Kalustyan's*. This emporium in Little India is brimming with items from around the world like spices, condiments, dried goods, cookwares, beauty products... the list is long. You'll need an extra suitcase.

imbibe / devour / covet:
bombay sandwich spread
lime & chili chutney
eucalyptus & linden honey
goan fish masala spice
syrian red pepper flakes
baby dark chick peas
black beluga lentils
2 cup pickle pot

king of falafel & shawarma

unsurpassed middle eastern food cart

30th street and broadway. n / w: broadway
718.838.8029 www.thekingfalafel.com
mon - sat 11a - 9p

opened in 2002. owner / chef: fares zeidaies
$: cash only
lunch. dinner. first come, first served

astoria > **e31**

JFD: It is, they say, good to be the king. It's also good to know the king. And if your path takes you by this fixture at 30th street in Astoria, you don't have a choice but to know the *King of Falafel & Shawarma*. Fares playfully calls out to all who pass by—mail carriers, working stiffs and loitering shifty characters. The smart ones head over and avail themselves of the intensely delicious fare. The smartest customer I saw was the stroller-bound toddler who demanded his mother roll him over to the King. For his efforts, he got a fresh falafel. "He's a regular," the King told me. I'm not surprised.

imbibe / devour:
sodas
chicken & rice platter
falafel wrap
kefta sandwiches
chicken shish kabobs
lamb chops
shawarma hero
king mean platter

lexington candy shop

old school, yummy lunch counter

1226 lexington avenue. corner of 83rd. 4 / 5 / 6: 86th street
212.288.0057 www.lexingtoncandyshop.com
mon - sat 7a - 7p sun 8a - 6p

opened in 1925. owner: john phillips
$-$$: visa. mc
lunch. dinner. treats. first come, first served

upper east side >

JH: At the risk of sounding cliché, *Lexington Candy Shop* is exactly what a New York City lunch counter should be. Diners sit on stools or in booths. Devil's food cakes are displayed on stands. The food is totally unfussy and satisfying. There are good ol' tuna melts or if you're intent on dieting, try the '70s version of the South Beach diet: a hamburger patty with cottage cheese and a lettuce leaf on the side. I was starting to wax nostalgic here, humming old standards by the Andrews Sisters when my waitress said, "Do you want another egg cream, sugar?" Whoa! Happy days are here again!

imbibe / devour:
fresh lime rickey
egg creams
cherry coke float
shrimp salad platter
fried egg sandwich
liverwurst sandwich
butterscotch sundae
miss gimble's cheesecake

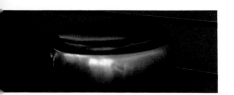

lucali

handthrown brick oven pizza
575 henry street. between carroll and first. f / g trains: carroll street
718.858.4086
wed - mon 6 - 10p

opened in 2006. owner / chef: mark iacono
$$: cash only
dinner. byob. first come, first served

carroll gardens > **e33**

JH: You never start praise with an apology, but here it goes anyway. I'm sorry that the photos of the uncommonly good pizza from *Lucali's* aren't better. They really should make your mouth water and command you to have inappropriate pizza fantasies. But because we don't use flash and this atmospheric room is lit only by candles (they even cook by candlelight), the pix are a bit moody. Maybe I was distracted by the perfect crust, or the chew and char of the pie was so dreamy that I drifted into some Italian fantasy and didn't get the shot. Whatever my sad excuse, don't miss *Lucali*.

imbibe / *devour:*
calzones
pizzas
toppings include:
  artichoke hearts
  basil
  pepperoni
  anchovies

lucas steakhouse

neighborhood steakhouse

34-55 32nd street. corner of 35th avenue. n / w: 36th avenue
718.786.5200 www.lucassteakhouse.com
tue - thur, sun 5 - 10:30p fri - sat 5 - 11:30p

opened in 2009. owner: johnny kolyenovic chef: carlos simoes
$$$: all major credit cards accepted
dinner. wine / beer. reservations accepted

long island city > e34

JFD: Steak is great, but steakhouses sometimes turn me off. It seems so much about volume that I envision a conveyor belt out back with mooing cows being transported in, falling into the hopper and then—clank, clatter, bam—being turned out onto the plate, right next to some creamed spinach. *Lucas* is nothing like this sordid vision. It's a neighborhood place, with choice, dry-aged beef, some great steakhouse essentials and an outrageously fun staff (ask the blond server to do his Christopher Walken impression). Though there are bigger name spots in town, *Lucas* satisfies with the best of them.

imbibe / devour:
05 chianti bello stento
saison dupont
clams casino
roasted beet salad
filet mignon carpaccio
ny strip au poivre
oven-roasted cornish hen
sautéed spanish onions

75

manducatis

old-school italian

1327 jackson avenue. between jackson and 47th. g: 21st avenue
718.729.4602 www.manducatis.com
mon - fri noon - 3p, 5 - 10p sat 5 - 11p sun 2:30 - 8p

opened in 1977. owner: vincenzo carbone chef: ida carbone
$$-$$$: all major credit cards accepted
lunch. dinner. full bar. reservations accepted

long island city > **e35**

CD: Call me a masochistic loon, but I like my Italian food cooked by stern Italian women and served to me by their slightly softer-edge Italian husbands. It's how the universe should work—which is why all is exactly as it should be at this near-ancient Long Island City haunt. Chef Ida cooks with a stone-cold poker face but a warm heart. Everyone in the room at *Manducatis*—and they've all been coming there for 20 years—knows Ida will cook the octopus to perfection and crank the spaghetti out herself. And if you order a Negroni from her husband Vincenzo? No need to worry about him scrimping on the gin.

imbibe / devour:
negroni
espresso
octopus with chickpeas & tomatoes
spaghetti with sun-dried tomatoes
pork chops alla paesana
tagliatelle with clams, tomatoes & cannelini beans
fettucine bolognese
cannoli

77

mast brothers chocolate

artisanal chocolate

105a north third street. between berry and wythe. l: bedford ave
718.388.2625 www.mastbrotherschocolate.com
mon - fri by chance sat - sun noon - 8p

opened in 2007. owners: rick and michael mast
$: cash only
treats. first come, first served

williamsburg >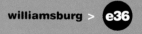

JFD: Have you ever seen a movie where the police stage a sting operation? They tell some dimwitted felons that they've won a big screen TV and tickets to a UFC cage match, and when the crooks show up to collect—it's slamma time. I've seen enough of these flicks that when I drew the coveted Williamsburg 'hood to cover for this book, meaning I'd get to visit *Mast Brothers*, I assumed I'd been set up. I mean, really? Handsome, musical, bearded men making artisanal, rigorously created and sourced chocolate in gorgeous packaging. Cuff me.

imbibe / devour:
dark chocolate, black truffles & sea salt bar
dark chocolate, pecans & maple syrup bar
dark chocolate, almonds & olive oil bar
dark chocolate & dried cranberries bar
fleur de sel bar
salt & pepper bar
cacao nibs
baking chocolate

mayahuel

abundant, high quality tequila and delicious mexican fare

304 east sixth street. between first and second avenues. 6: astor place
212.253.5888 www.mayahuelny.com tw: @mayahuelny
mon - sat 6p - 2a sun 2p - midnight

opened in 2009. owners: philip ward and ravi derossi chef: luis gonzales
$$-$$$: all major credit cards accepted
dinner. brunch. full bar. first come, first served

east village >

JFD: To be aged and rested sounds alright to me. You'll find these two categories of sipping tequila—"anejo" and "reposado"—at *Mayahuel*, along with dozens of younger, rarer and somewhat exotic relatives of the Mexican liquor. Obviously this is a place for agave enthusiasts. The rest of us, who don't exactly qualify as enthusiasts, who identify more as "never drinking tequila again until I can restore my dignity following those 36 lost hours in Phoenix and/or until I find that rental car" might be excited about the seriously delicious Mexican food here and a nice beer or two.

imbibe / devour:
dozens of tequilas & mezcals
beer cocktails
popcorn with lime, cotija cheese & ancho chili
braised pork belly with papaya mango mustard
mole braised chicken tamales
hangar steak over summer corn pudding
chilaquiles
tres leches

81

mercat negre

romantic setting for catalan small plates

65 grand street. between wythe and kent. l: bedford avenue
347.223.4599 www.mercatnegre.com tw: @mercatnegre
see website for hours

opened in 2009. owner: jaime reixach chef: oriol sala colomer
$$-$$$: cash only
lunch. dinner. brunch. full bar. first come, first served

williamsburg > 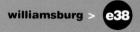 **e38**

JFD: I will eat through anything—anything—if you promise me that there's a delicious socorat to be found at the bottom of dish. That crunchy layer of rice found in paellas transforms me from mild-mannered diner to crazed junkie. The fantastic thing about *Mercat Negre* is that their paella's layers—comprised of cuttelfish, rabbit and pork—are almost as delectable as the socorat, thanks to Oriol, *Mercat's* El Bulli-trained chef. I like to think of these layers as foreplay before the big event. Follow your paella (or any of the other amazing dishes here) with a dessert or, perhaps, a cigarette.

imbibe / devour:
08 muga rioja
08 galiciano valdeorras, godello
death in spain cocktail
deep-fried & breaded baby octopus
bomba rice with cuttlefish & blackened onions
duck cheeseburger
toasted bread with olive oil, chocolate & salt
lemon frappe

milk bar

a convivial neighborhood café

620 vanderbilt avenue. corner of prospect. b / q: seventh avenue
718.230.0844 www.milkbarbrooklyn.com
mon - fri 7:30a - 6p sat - sun 9a - 6p

opened in 2009. owners: alexander hall and sabrina godfrey chef: alexander hall
$-$$: cash only
breakfast. lunch. brunch. treats. wine / beer. first come, first served

prospect heights > **e39**

JFD: Wellies. Gits. Snog. Chuffed. All words that make me smile for no particular reason. Add to those, toasties. It's a twee little word, and when I saw them featured on the menu at *Milk Bar*, I knew I liked this place. As it happens, the whole vibe here is happy-making. I smiled my way through an entire breakfast as I watched Prospect Heights families come and go, all of whom also seemed delighted that this Australian-inspired café had suddenly materialized among them. I know I sound like a nutter when I talk this way, but it's a spiffing good place.

imbibe / devour:
australian iced coffee
yuengling beer
avocado toast
dub pie of the day
cold rice sandwich
poached seasonal fruits
salami baguette
toastie

mimi's hummus

charming middle-eastern spot

1209 cortelyou road. between westminster and argyle. q: cortelyou road
718.284.4444 www.mimishummus.com
mon - fri noon - 10:30p fri - sat 11a - 11p sun 11a - 10:30p

opened in 2009. owners: mimi kitani and avi shuker
$-$$: visa. mc
dinner. lunch. first come, first served

ditmas park > **e40**

AB: Time is at a premium in this city, where the term "bustling with energy" is a laughable understatement. So who has the time to leave his or her own sphere to eat? This was the question on my mind when I trekked to Ditmas Park to eat at *Mimi's Hummus*. Would anybody in their right (i.e., harried) mind make this trip for hummus? The answer is yes. I would happily have flown halfway around the world to Israel to eat this food. So slow down for a moment and remind yourself that a quick trip on the Q train is well worth it for a little bit of hummus heaven.

imbibe / devour:
fresh mint & sage tea
turkish coffee
masabache hummus
fava bean hummus
shakshuka eggs
stuffed grape leaves
eggplant caviar
housemade cookies

miss mamie's spoonbread too

southern cooking

366 west 110th street. between columbus and manhattan
b / c: cathedral parkway-110th street
212.865.6744 www.spoonbreadinc.com/miss_mamies.htm
mon - sun 11:30a - 10p

opened in 1999. owner: norma darden chefs: jason lloyd and steve cox
$-$$: all major credit cards accepted
brunch. lunch. dinner. wine / beer. first come, first served

harlem >

CD: Fried chicken. Blackeyed peas. Collard greens. It's all at *Miss Mamie's*, and it's all very, very good. But it's made even better by the cheery green and yellow tiled floor. And the checkered table cloths. And the red velvet cake perched on a glass cake stand, waiting for someone to slice into it. And the sunny disposition that *Miss Mamie's* embodies. Sure it's a little over the top, but after a day spent wandering the streets of Harlem and Morningside Heights, nothing feels more like coming home than digging into a plate of good old-fashioned Southern food. You're in good hands.

imbibe / devour:
sweetened iced tea
harlem brewing company sugar hill golden ale
miss mamie's sampler
louisiana catfish
homemade meatloaf
hoppin' john
macaroni & cheese
sweet potato pie

mitchell's soul food

no frills, real deal food

617a vanderbilt avenue. between bergen and st. marks. 2 / 3: grand army plaza
718.789.3212
wed - fri 10a - 10:30p sat noon - 10:30p sun 1 - 8p

opened about 25 years ago. owner / chef: jb bromell
$: cash only
breakfast. lunch. dinner. free delivery. first come, first served

prospect heights > e42

KW: We all know that it's dangerous to drive while tired, but I find that it's also tricky to write while tired. There are the obvious downfalls like writing a whole blurb, then realizing that you've said nothing about nothing. Though I'm tired right now from a late-night writing session, I am clear as a bell when it comes to this. *Mitchell's* has the best damn fried chicken in Brooklyn. Though this unassuming place could be easily passed by on the street, JB's soul food is the bomb. He cooks everything himself and often acts as waitstaff, too. If only I could have a piece of his chicken now I'd be revived.

imbibe / devour:
homemade sweet tea
homemade lemonade
fried chicken
smothered chicken
tomatoes & okra
blackeyed peas
chitterlings
coconut pie

no.7

not easily definable food

7 greene avenue. corner of fulton. c: lafayette
718.522.6370 www.no7restaurant.com
see website for hours

opened in 2008. owners: a guy named matt and a guy named tyler
chef: the tyler guy
$$-$$$: visa. mc
lunch. dinner. brunch. full bar. reservations accepted for parties of six or more

fort greene > **e43**

KW: While I was at *No.7*, I spent some time chatting with Matt, one of the owners. I was being a bit cheeky when I asked why he and Tyler, the chef, didn't open a turn-of-the-century, Americana-esque spot. He gave me, rightfully so, the stink-eye as these guys follow the beat of their own drum—which I heartily applaud. The food here is damn hard to categorize, but here's my stab: American meets Korean with a dash of Spanish flair. Most importantly, it's insanely delicious. And now there's *No.7 Sub* at The Ace Hotel where their signature flair will be applied to the food du jour: sandwiches.

imbibe / devour:
cucumber, thyme, rye & herb sainte
mint sun tea with bourbon & lemon
cold grilled octopus
pumpkin seed crusted tofu
chicken stuffed cabbage
grilled wagyu bavette steak
sweet corn french toast
brown butter pudding

93

northern spy food co.

local and regional good stuff

511 east 12th street. between a and b. l: first avenue > f / v: second avenue
212.228.5100 www.northernspyfoodco.com tw: @northernspyfood
sun - thu 11a - 11p fri - sat 11a - midnight

opened in 2009. owner / chef: nathan foot owners: chris ronis and christophe hille
$$: all major credit cards accepted
breakfast. lunch. dinner. brunch. grocery. wine / beer. first come, first served

east village >

JFD: Back when I lived in Brooklyn, a sign appeared one day on a neighboring building announcing "The Vermont Store." I got really excited, imagining the fresh maple syrup and delicious cheeses I'd have access to. Instead, the guy sold hairspray, Christmas trees and maps. Major letdown. What I wanted is what *Northern Spy* is: a provisioner that makes and sells only small batch and artisanal foods from New York and New England. Honeys, syrups, pickles, milk, cheese, jams—all the good stuff. And there's a restaurant, too. It's all here in this little rural part of the East Village.

imbibe / devour:
quince seltzer
bluepoint oatmeal stout
red bean puree
pork terrine
squid & mussels
roasted chicken
stewed runner beans
apple pie with almond semifreddo

peaches

modern southern fare

393 lewis avenue. between macdonough and decatur. a / c: utica avenue
718.942.4162 www.peachesbrooklyn.com
see website for hours

opened in 2008. owners: ben grossman and craig samuel
chef: damian laverty-mcdowell
$$: all major credit cards accepted
lunch. dinner. brunch. full bar. first come, first served

bedford-stuyvesant >

KW: A while back, my brother and I were discussing comfort food. He said his favorite was apples. Apples?? I'm still scratching my head over this. In my mind, comfort food is warm and filling and a little naughty. In my food vernacular, this means meatloaf, mac and cheese and pie—basically the food that is made at *Peaches*, but with an urban flair. I suggest sidling up to the bar where the über-charming Ron rules the roost. Have him pour you a brownstone punch then dig into something homey like the pulled pork and grits. If you're not comforted by the end of your meal, I'll eat my words.

imbibe / devour:
brownstone punch
watermelon martini
harlem brewing sugar hill ale
market vegetable salad
turkey meatloaf sandwich
hand-dipped flounder
12-hour smoked short ribs
wilklow farms country pies

philoxenia

tasteful greek dining

3207 34th avenue. between 32nd and 33rd. n / w: broadway
718.626.2000 www.philoxeniarestaurant.com
tue - fri 4 -11p sat - sun 1 - 11p

opened in 2004. owner / chef: dionysia germani owner: antonis manolas
$$: all major credit cards accepted
dinner. full bar. first come, first served

astoria >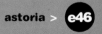

JFD: My only trip to Greece in the '90s yielded many firsts. My first time hitchhiking, eating whole fish, snorkeling, rapping the floor with my knuckles while shouting "*opa!*" and drinking retsina (okay, it was the first time I went to an Ikea also, but that's a random aside). With so many memorable firsts concentrated in one short visit, I've always felt a connection to the country. So now when I eat at a Greek restaurant, I want that connection validated by friendly, hospitable folk who will remind me of that amazing trip. That's exactly what I found at *Philoxenia*, along with whole fish and retsina. *Kalh orexh.*

imbibe / devour:
05 gaia estate assyrtiko, thalassitis
05 katogi-averoff, epirus
pan-fried graviera cheese
beets with skordalia
grilled bronzini
baked eggplant rolls stuffed with feta
grilled shrimp with ladolemono dressing
fresh custard cream wrapped in phyllo

porchetta

slow-cooked italian fast food

110 east seventh street. between first and a. 6: astor place > f / v: second avenue
212.777.2151 www.porchettanyc.com tw: @porchettanyc
sun - thu 11:30a - 10p fri - sat 11:30a - 11p

opened in 2008. owner / chef: sara jenkins owner: matthew lindemulder
$-$$: visa. mc
lunch. dinner. first come, first served

east village >

JFD: In Italy, porchetta is hawked out of white vans, which the locals, if they have any sense, chase down the street like kids pursuing a Mr. Softee truck. Just reading about porchetta gets me salivating. In three Wikipedia sentences, these words appear: "savory, fatty, moist, deboned, meat, fat, crispy skin, rolled, spitted, roasted over wood, heavily salted, stuffed, garlic, rosemary, fennel, wild herbs." I swear I'm not too lazy to write my own blurb; I just don't think I could improve on that. Better than reading is going to the tiny (8 or so seats up for grabs) *Porchetta*, where Sara's pork is *molto bene*.

imbibe / devour:
lemonade
boylston sodas
porchetta sandwich
slow-cooked pork ragu with grilled ciabatta
pumpkin soup
chicory salad with garlic dressing
crispy potatoes & burnt ends
biscotti

prime meats

it's all about the meat

465 court street. corner of luquer. f / g: carroll street
718.254.0327 www.frankspm.com
see website for hours

opened in 2009. owner / chefs: frank falcinelli and frank castronovo
$$: cash only
breakfast. lunch. dinner. full bar. reservations recommended

carroll gardens > **e48**

JH: Meat is all the rage again! This is good news for us omnivores but less so for the relatives of my childhood pet cow, Big Buns, though I will say that times have improved for BB's ilk. All of this attention to meat and its provenance means the bovines of to-day are being raised in the best conditions and being fed the finest foods. At *Prime Meats*, the crack team behind the beloved *Frankies Sputino* brings the same care and flair to the steakhouse concept but make it interesting with a German / Austrian twist. Big Buns would be so proud.

imbibe / devour:
weinenstephan hefeweiss
'06 chateau de chorey bourgogne
celery salad
landjäger
the vesper brett - alpine tasting board
36 day dry-aged bone in ribeye
herb & wild mushroom spätzle
linzer torte

roberta's

wood-fired pizza

261 moore street. between white and bogart streets. l: morgan avenue
718.417.1118 www.robertaspizza.com
mon - fri noon - midnight sat - sun 11a - midnight

opened in 2008. owners: chris parachini and brandon hoy chef: carlo mirarchi
$$: all major credit cards accepted
lunch. dinner. brunch. wine / beer. first come, first served

bushwick >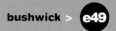

CD: Bushwick may be a trendy neighborhood in Brooklyn, but I still consider any business that opens up there a modern-day frontier outpost. Maybe it's the piles of firewood that greet you when you walk into *Roberta's* or the saloon-like feel of the bar or the fact that all the men have beards—but it feels pretty much like the Wild West. Of course there's the simplicity of the food to take into consideration—wood-fired pizzas, grilled skirt steak, roasted marrow bones—all of which makes this place the sort of joint I'd want to come upon after a long ride on the urban range.

imbibe / devour:
fresh mint lemonade
juan benegas malbec
snapperhead ipa
romanesco salad with pistachio butter & lardo
roasted veal marrow bones with grilled bread
good girl pizza
specken wolf pizza
grilled skirt steak

roman's

fresh, cozy italian fare

243 dekalb avenue. between vanderbilt and clermont
g: clinton-washington
718.622.5300 www.romansnyc.com
tue - thu 5 - 11p sat - sun 5p - midnight

opened in 2009. owners: mark firth and andrew tarlow chef: david gould
$$-$$$: all major credit cards accepted
dinner. full bar. first come, first served

fort greene > **e50**

JFD: Rome wasn't built in a day, and *Roman's* didn't just spring forth in one day (nor did it emerge from a giant wolf). In fact, the owners cut their teeth on the imperative Williamsburg spots *Marlow & Sons* and *Diner*, a hop, skip and a BQE away, before creating this fresh Italian restaurant. But it's here now, and I'm happy to report that I veni, vidi, eati, drinki. Especially memorable was the chitarra: chewy, tender strips of pasta formed on a guitar-string frame and served with clean tomato sauce. Yum. Lend me your ears, countrymen, and let me suggest that you check out *Roman's,* too.

imbibe / devour:
daily bitters
menabrea blonde
crostini with anchovy & salsa verde
shaved hubbard squash with almonds & olives
pasta chitarra with tomato & raw cow cheese
tilefish with celery root & charred lemon
sautéed tatsoi
chocolate sorbet

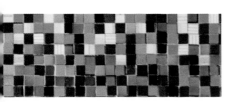

107

saltie

inventive sandwiches and market fresh dishes

378 metropolitan avenue. between marcy and havemeyer. l: bedford avenue
718.387.4777 www.saltieny.com tw: @saltieny
tue - sun 10a - 8p

opened in 2009
owner / chefs: caroline fidanza, rebecca collerton and elizabeth schula
$-$$: cash only
breakfast. lunch. dinner. brunch. first come, first served

williamsburg > e51

JFD: Don't blame me if this whole blurb ends up in pirate speak. Blame the owners of *Saltie*. They're the ones who named the sandwiches "Scuttlebutt" and "the Captain's Daughter" and put up signage indicating "it's a tight ship" in this galley-sized take-out shop. But, avast, me hearty, if yar looking for sandwiches featurin' uncommon ingredients, in big heaps of bountiful freshness, set your compass for here. Actually, there's much more to this place than sandwiches, including scrumptious pastries and rich ice cream desserts. Landlubbers and food lovers welcome.

imbibe / devour:
plum cardamom lassi
aqua fresco
the scuttlebutt
ship's biscuit
clean slate
potato tortilla
eccles cake
ice cream sandwich

saraghina

neapolitan pizza in a stylish, vintage environment
435 halsey street. corner of lewis. c: kingston-throop
daily 6 - 11p

opened in 2009. owners: edoardo mantelli and massimiliano nanni
\$-\$\$: cash only
dinner. first come, first served

bedford-stuyvesant > **e52**

AB: At the start of our work on this book, Jan and I were in the throes of distress and had a mutual bad case of the grumpies. Then we went to *Saraghina*, and our attitudes took a turn for the better. Suddenly the world was golden and everything was wonderful. We were so taken by *Saraghina* and its divine pizza that we considered moving down the street in Bed-Stuy so we could commune daily with the regulars—from folks newly moved to the neighborhood to those who had spent their whole lives here. The mix was infectious, and the food was dee-lish-us.

imbibe / *devour:*
house red wine
pizzas:
  margherita
  bufalo
  prosciutto & funghi
  capocollo
burratina
tagliatelle al ragu

sunrise mart

japanese specialty market

494 broome street. between wooster and broadway. c / e: spring street
4 stuyvesant street, second floor. at third. 6: astor place
212.219.0033
mon - fri 10a - 10p   fri - sat 10a - midnight

opened in 1994
$-$$: all major credit cards accepted
light meals. grocery. first come, first served

soho / east village > 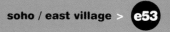 e53

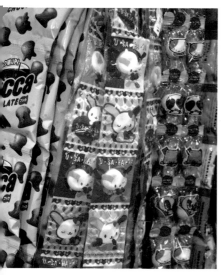

AB: I've come up with a new diet—The Japanese Candy diet. I want to clarify immediately that this concept is slightly different than the idea of *hara hachi bunme*, which is eating until you are about 80 percent full. My Japanese Candy diet is based off of a daily intake of the type of treats that one can find at *Sunrise Mart*: Pucca chocolate, Yim-Yam, yuzu gummies, milk candies—and it is imperative to make yourself gloriously, 100% full. This will then create a healthy glow of sugar satisfaction. If you don't believe in the brilliance of my diet, you can also grab a bento box here or a multitude of Asian groceries.

imbibe / devour:
pokari sweat drink
green tea with brown rice
otokomae tofu
sticky rice
pink salt
udon noodles
beautifully packaged soy sauce
extensive rice variety

the breslin

high-end english pub fare

16 west 29th street (in the ace hotel). between broadway and fifth
r / w: 28th street
212.679.1939 www.thebreslin.com
see website for hours

opened in 2009. owner / executive chef: april bloomfield owner: ken friedman
$$-$$$: all major credit cards accepted
breakfast. lunch. dinner. full bar. first come, first served

murray hill / gramercy park > **e54**

JFD: Location, location, location. *The Breslin* is situated in a confluence of neighborhoods, where Gramercy Park begins to meet the Flatiron District. But that's not the location I speak of. *The Breslin* can also be located directly below your bed. Situated on the ground floor of the of-the-moment Ace Hotel, you need only hail an elevator to experience April's British haute comfort food that honors "nose-to-tail" thinking. Staycation is still a goofy word, but if this spot with its UK provenance, by way of the Pacific Northwest, as interpreted in New York style, is your destination—what a great itinerary.

imbibe / devour:
the breslin bloody mary
hot cross buns
full english breakfast
blood sausage with eggs & creamy tarragon
beef & stilton pie
fried head cheese with sauce gribiche
braised shin of beef with black cabbage
eton mess

the farm on adderley

farm-fresh, seasonal ingredients

1108 cortelyou road. between 11th and 12th. q: cortelyou road
718.287.3101 www.thefarmonadderley.com
see website for hours

opened in 2006. owner: gary jonas chef: tom kearney
$$: all major credit cards accepted
breakfast. lunch. dinner. brunch. reservations accepted for parties of five or more

ditmas park > e55

AB: Over the last couple of years, the locavore movement has taken hold of New York City, especially in Brooklyn where urban farmers are digging up their tiny backyards (if they are lucky enough to have one) to grow vegetables and raise chickens. Though this sounds idyllic, let's be frank—there are not a lot of people living in the city who have the resources to do this. So what to do if you're hankering to eat farm-fresh food? Easy. Just amble over to *The Farm on Adderley*. Everything here is hand-chosen from local purveyors, and the food is simple, homey and downright delicious. Yee-haw.

imbibe / devour:
ommegang abbey
six point apollo wheat ale
grilled eggplant toast
hens of the wood mushroom tempura
pan-roasted pollack
short rib ravioli
farm burger
french fries with curry mayo

the hungarian pastry shop

old-world bakery and cafe

1030 amsterdam avenue. between 110th and 111th
1: cathedral pkwy-110th street
212.866.4230
mon - fri 7:30a - 11p sat 8:30a - 11:30p sun 8:30a - 10:30p

opened in 1961. owner: panagiotis binioris
$: cash only
treats. first come, first served

morningside heights > **e56**

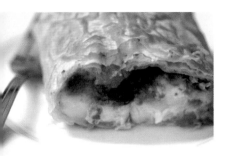

IN CASE OF FIRE
Keep Calm
Pay Bill
Then Run

CD: The first time I visited Europe, I didn't go to France or Italy. I went to Hungary on a work trip. And though it had never crossed my mind to travel there, I fell deeply in love with the place, in large part because of the dobos torte—a luscious five-layer sponge cake interspersed with chocolate buttercream and crunchy caramel—served in just about every café in Budapest. Though *The Hungarian Pastry Shop* is much more rustic than the opulent dessert shops of Budapest, eating the dobos torte at this funky, old world spot felt just as luxurious.

imbibe / devour:
cappuccino
viennese coffee
marzipan cake
seven-layer pyramid cake
rigo jansci chocolate cake
cherry & cheese strudel
sacher torte
dobos torte

STRUDEL
By the lb.
or
Slice served

the redhead

southern gothic restaurant and bar

349 east 13th street. between first and second. l: first avenue > 6: 14th street
212.533.6212 www.theredheadnyc.com
see website for hours

opened in 2008. owner / chef: meg grace owners: gregg nelson and rob larcom
$$: all major credit cards accepted
dinner. brunch. full bar. first come, first served

east village > **e57**

JFD: You'd think that the promise of bacon peanut brittle would be what lured me to *The Redhead*. Good guess, but wrong. What first enticed me was learning that this restaurant had originally opened as a bar, become a fixture in the 'hood, and then gently transitioned into a fine, southern-inflected restaurant, home to some killer crispy buttermilk chicken. So, it was the "bar done good story" that got me in the door. Then a series of bayou-inspired dishes rooted me to my seat. And the chocolate car bomb at dinner's end—that just dropped me to the floor.

imbibe / devour:
ommegang rare vos
sazerac
soft pretzel with kentucky beer cheese
one-eyed caesar salad
creamy parsnip soup with poached lobster
low country shrimp
buttermilk fried chicken
caramel banana pudding

the ten bells

natural wines, oysters and small plates

247 broome street. between orchard and ludlow
f / m / z: essex - delancy streets
212.228.4450 www.thetenbells.com
mon - fri 5p - 2a sat - sun 3p - 2a

opened in 2008. owner: fifi essome chef: javier ortega
$$: cash only
dinner. wine / beer. first come, first served

lower east side > e58

JH: I love wine; I just hate talking about it. I would rather drink beer than have to discuss the "chewiness" of a Cabernet Franc. I find that level of fanaticism comparable to a Dungeons and Dragons obsession. This is why I love *The Ten Bells*. Not only are the wines excellent (they only serve natural wines), the atmosphere is like a lively bistro rather than a room filled with gamers dourly discussing wizard leveling guides. And the staff, though incredibly knowledgeable, doesn't seem to take themselves too seriously because they've got better things to do like shuck me a dozen of those delicious oysters.

imbibe / devour:
06 arbois pupillin melon
08 wurtz "cuvee 10 bells" riesling
malpeque oysters
papas bravas
potato & octopus salad
boquerones
hand-cut tartare
chocolate cigars

txikito

cocina vasca

240 ninth avenue. between 24th and 25th. c / e: 23rd avenue
www.txikitonyc.com
lunch tue - fri noon - 3p dinner tue - thu, sun 5 - 11p fri - sat 5p - midnight

opened in 2008. owner / chefs: alexandra raij and eder montero
$$: all major credit cards accepted
lunch. dinner. first come, first served

chelsea > 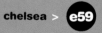 **e59**

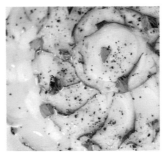

KW: When I lived in Chelsea during my college years, I used to think that the little retail strip on Ninth Avenue near 23rd would be a great place for a restaurant. Twenty or so years later, the folks at *Txikito* saw the same promise and planted their Basque roots here (as did Jim Lahey, whose great pizza spot *Co.* is on the corner). So I planted myself at the bar and proceeded to order paper thin slices of octopus and triangles of breaded tongue with cornichon slices. After eating I felt slightly depressed. The food was incredibly good, but what a downer that I no longer lived in this neighborhood so I could eat here every night.

imbibe / devour:
farnum hill "basque-style" cider
elkano cocktail
foie micuit
arraultza
pulpo
morcilla
lengua
txilindron

vanessa's dumpling house

delicious little dumplings made by talented little hands.

118a eldridge street. between grand and broome. b / d: grand street
212.625.8008
mon - sat 7:30a - 10:30p sun 7:30a - 10p

opened in 2001. owner: vanessa weng
$: all major credit cards accepted
lunch. dinner. treats. first come, first served

lower east side >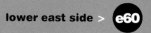

JH: Supposedly New York is one of the most expensive cities in the world. And yes, my jaw has dropped at the sight of some of my restaurant tabs. But even frugal *moi* can't understand how it's possible to have such an awesome meal at *Vanessa's Dumpling House* for such a low price. Is Vanessa a secret millionaire who makes dumplings for pure pleasure, not monetary gain? If I'm right, it's all the more reason to thank her for some of the best, most inspired dumplings in this city. And don't forget to have the sesame pancake sandwich, which is akin to a chewy Asian panino, and did I mention, cheap?!

imbibe / devour:
honeydew milk tea
date honey
sesame pancake with egg sandwich
cabbage & pork fried dumplings
pork fried buns
fish ball noodle soup
sour & spicy cucumber
roasted pork noodle soup

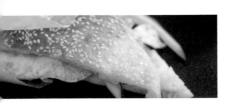

127

van leeuwen artisan ice cream

ice cream and coffee worth searching for

632 manhattan avenue. at bedford and nassau. g: nassau > l: bedford
also truck moves around manhattan and brooklyn
718.701.1630 www.vanleeuwenicecream.com tw: @vlaic
see website / twitter for hours and locations

opened in 2008. owner / chef: ben van leeuwen
owners: peter and laura o'neil
$-$$: cash only
coffee / tea. treats. first come, first served

greenpoint / various locations > **e61**

JFD: I drove an ice cream truck during the summer in high school. I sped around trolling for kids, blasting Billy Idol in an effort to drown out the Joplin-esque calliope music. It was hell on earth. As you might imagine, I don't take too kindly to ice cream trucks. But *Van Leeuwen* charmed me. Concentrating on making just a handful of ice creams really well, and turning out killer coffee, this family doesn't need to play foul jingles to attract (or repel) a crowd. The truck simply appears on certain Brooklyn and Manhattan street corners, and the people come. And right as this book was going to press, they opened a storefront!

imbibe / devour:
intelligentsia coffee
pastries & jellies
ice creams:
  vanilla
  chocolate
  red currant
  pistachio
  giandujia

village tart

savory and sweet

86 kenmare street. corner of mott. 6: prince > j / m: bowery
212.226.4980 www.villagetart.com tw: @villagetart
sun - wed 8a - midnight thu - sat 8a - 2a

opened in 2010. owners: lesly bernard and pat suh
chefs: janina amezcua and pichet ong
$$: all major credit cards accepted
breakfast. lunch. dinner. brunch. coffee / tea. treats. first come, first served

nolita >

KW: One of my favorite memories from childhood is going shopping with my mother and grandparents. While my mother and grandmother went happily from store to store, my grandfather Red and I would shuffle along, getting less enthusiastic by the moment. Then, with his trademark twinkle, he would announce, "It's time for some sustenance." This was the moment I was waiting for—when we would sit down and have a treat. If Red were alive today, we would come to *Village Tart* and revive, whatever hour of the day, and he would had the Meyer lemon meringue. Here's to sustenance.

imbibe / devour:
caramel lassi
single origin drip coffee
chocolate nutella cake
grapefruit curd & almond frangipane
village alfajor
candied apple galette
peking duck pizzeta
wagyu beef franks in blanket

131

vinegar hill house

vintage ambience and wood-fired cooking

72 hudson avenue. between front and water streets
f: york street > a: high street
718.522.1018 www.vinegarhillhouse.com
see website for hours

opened in 2008. owner / executive chef: jean adamson owner: sam buffa
$$: all major credit cards accepted
dinner. brunch. full bar. first come, first served

vinegar hill >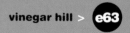

JFD: I research long and hard before I ever set foot in a place, and then I research some more. Getting rid of the industry jargon, this means I eat and drink a lot. And I get giddy when my choices are validated. Sometimes this validation comes from within: the food is fantastic and I love the place. Sometimes the validation comes when I mention a restaurant to others whose judgment I trust, and they heartily concur. Other times it's because the press gushes in droves about the place. All of this is true of *Vinegar Hill House*. This city loves this restaurant, and I can validate the affection.

imbibe / devour:
highland cocktail
basque apple cider
bitter green salad
oven-roasted octopus
pork rib cannelloni
cast-iron chicken
red wattle country chop
guinness chocolate cake

xie xie

killer asian sandwiches

645 west ninth avenue. between 45th and 46th. a / c / e: 42nd street
212.265.2975 www.xiexieproject.com tw: @xiexieproject
mon - sun 11:30a - 8:30p

opened in 2009. owner / chef: angelo sosa
$-$$: all major credit cards accepted
lunch. dinner. treats. wine / beer. delivery. first come, first served

hell's kitchen > 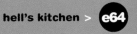 **e64**

JFD: I'd eaten day-old bread, bacon-of-the-month and past-its-due-date cream cheese. But I'd never ever had a 1,000-year-old ice cream sandwich until I went to *Xie Xie*. And you could certainly say it was worth the wait. It isn't truly a millennium-old dessert, as advertised, but a clever homage to the popular Asian egg dish. And while the sweet sandwich, with its gooey black caramel is something spectacular, it is the savory sandwiches that make this place extra special. You don't have to wait even 1,000 seconds for one of them. Go get one this minute—or have it delivered. Instant happiness.

imbibe / devour:
tumai water
tiger beer
sweet glazed pork sandwich
fish cha ca la vong
asian lobster roll
shredded chicken salad with truffle dressing
xie xie fortune cookie
1,000-year-old ice cream sandwich

zibetto

italian espresso bar

102 fulton street. between william and dutch. 2 / 3 / 4 / 5 / j / z / m: fulton street
1385 sixth avenue. between 56th and 57th. b / d / e: seventh avenue
www.zibetto.com
mon - fri 7a - 7p sat 9a - 5p sun 10a - 4p

opened in 2008. owners: hacene bouaroudj and anastasios nougos
$: cash only
coffee / tea. treats. first come, first served

financial district / midtown westside >

CD: As a West Coaster, I know that coffee culture dictates one must order a cup of coffee from a bearded barista, sit down with a laptop and remain seated for at least three hours. But nearly a decade spent living in NYC rendered me way too neurotic and high speed to ever embrace this lifestyle. Hence, walking into *Zibetto* felt like coming home. The man behind the counter wore a crisp white button-up and a tie and was clean shaven. And his cappuccinos and marocchinos? Inspired works of art. Customers stand at the counter while they imbibe, but they don't linger. They have better things to do.

imbibe / devour:
cappuccino
hot chocolate
marocchino
affogato al caffe
aranciata
italian croissant
almond biscotti
caprese sandwich

brooklyn:
tmas park
midwood

eat

e40 > mimi's hummus
> the farm on adderley
e15 > di fara pizza

shop

s47 > sacred vibes

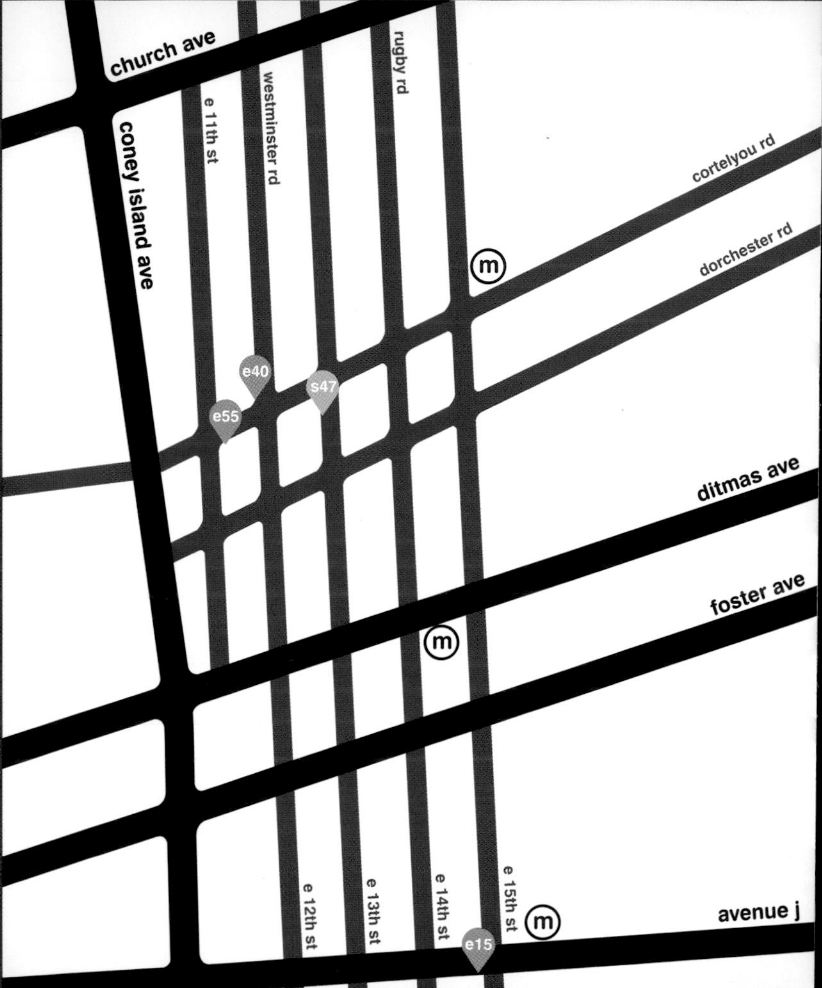

brooklyn:
red hook •

eat

e10 > botanica
e22 > fort defiance
e26 > home/made

shop

s17 > erie basin
s20 > foxy & winston
s37 > metal & thread
s48 > saipua

all maps face north

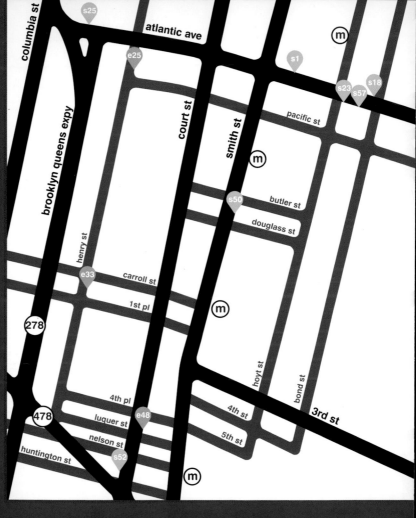

brooklyn:
- **boerum hill**
- **cobble hill**
- **carroll gardens**

eat

e25 > henry public
e33 > lucali
e48 > prime meats

shop

s1 > acorn
s18 > eva gentry
s23 > hollander & lexer
s25 > holler & squall
s50 > smith + butler
s52 > store 518
s57 > the banquet

note: all maps face r

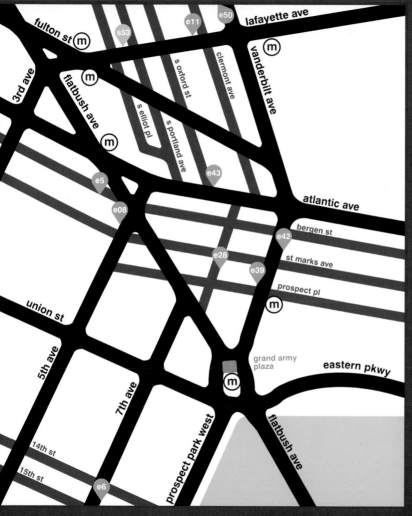

brooklyn:
park slope •
prospect heights •
clinton hill •
fort greene •

eat

e5 > bark hot dogs
e6 > beer table
e8 > bklyn larder
e11 > brooklyn flea
e28 > james
e39 > milk bar
e42 > mitchell's soul food
e43 > no.7
e50 > roman's

shop

s53 > stuart & wright

all maps face north

brooklyn:
• bedford - stuyvesant

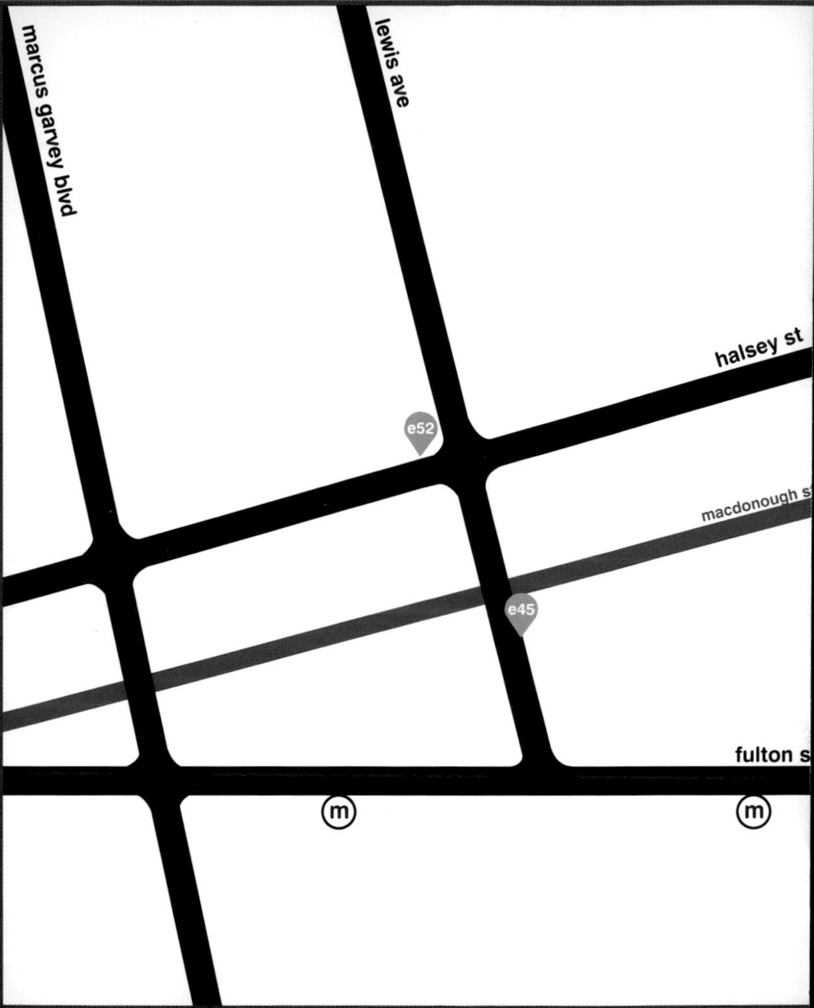

marcus garvey blvd
lewis ave
halsey st
macdonough st
e52
e45
fulton s
m
m

eat

e45 > peaches
e52 > saraghina

note: all maps face

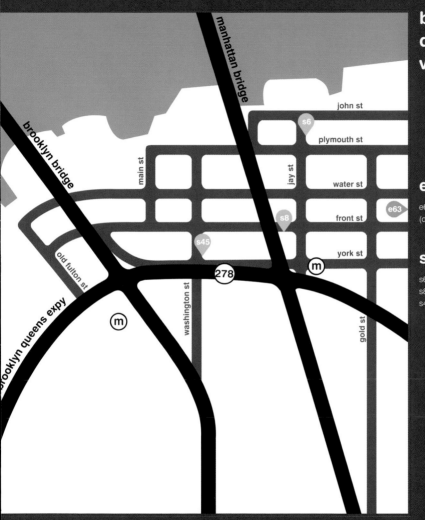

brooklyn:
dumbo •
vinegar hil

eat

e63 > vinegar hill house
(off map)

shop

s6 > baxter & liebchen
s8 > blueberi
s45 > pomme

brooklyn:
- ## williamsburg
- ## bushwick

eat

e36 > mast brothers chocolate
e38 > mercat negre
e49 > roberta's
e51 > saltie

shop

s11 > brook farm general store
s29 > jumelle
s54 > sweet william
s61 > voos

eat

e62 > van leeuwen artisan ice cream

shop

s30 > kill devil hill
s33 > le grenier

all maps face north

queens:
long island
city

eat

e19 > dutch kills
e35 > manducatti's

vernon blvd

11th st

21st st

queensboro bridge

59th st bridge

e19

(m)

dutch kill st

46th rd

ps1
contemporary
art center

47th ave

e35

47th rd

thomson ave

(m)

jackson ave

495

queens midtown expy

eat

e31 > king of falafel
& shawarma
34 > lucas steakhouse
e46 > philoxenia

shop

s49 > site

all maps face north

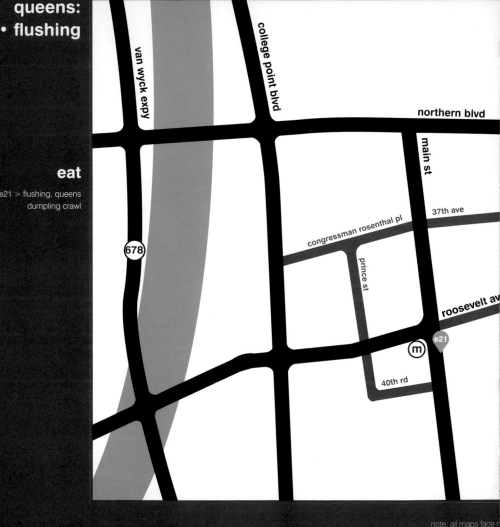

eat

van wyck expy

college point blvd

northern blvd

main st

37th ave

congressman rosenthal pl

678

prince st

roosevelt av

e21

m

40th rd

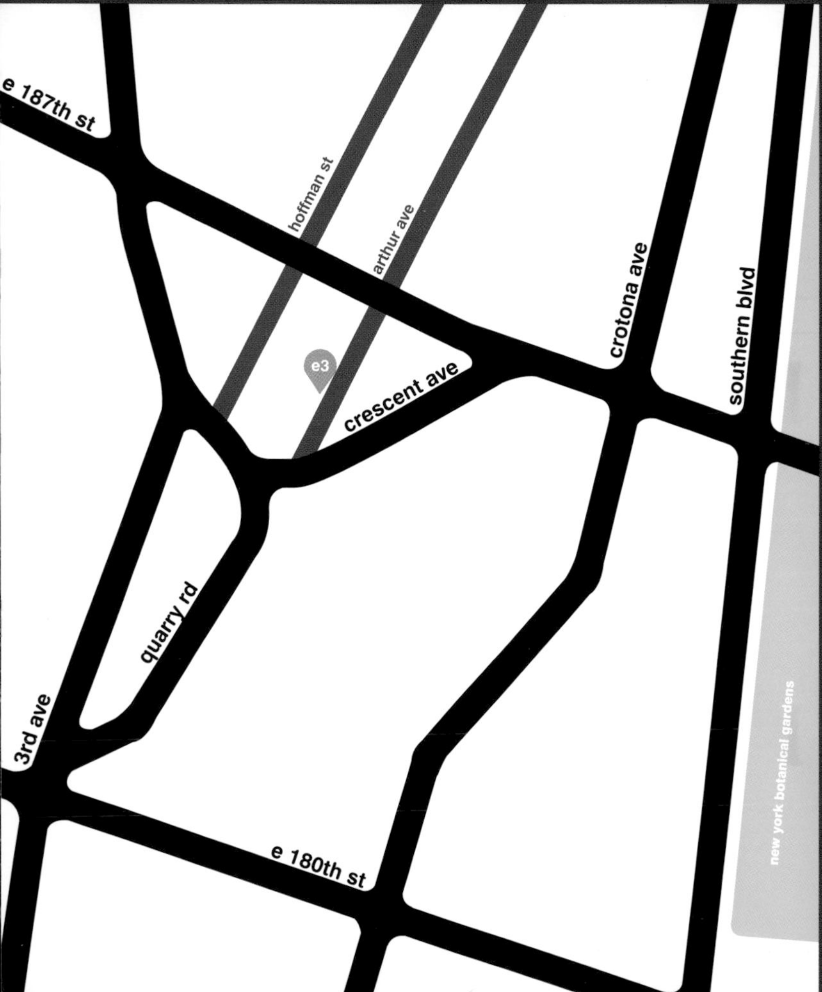
e 187th st
hoffman st
arthur ave
crotona ave
southern blvd
e3
crescent ave
quarry rd
3rd ave
new york botanical gardens
e 180th st

bronx: belmont •

eat

e3 > arthur avenue

e: all maps face north

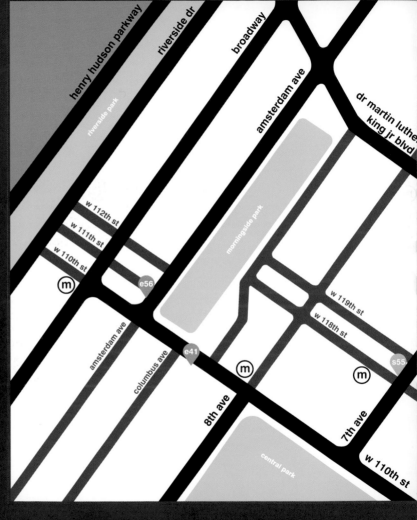

manhattan:
- **harlem**
- **morningside heights**

eat

e41 > miss mamie's spoonbread too

e56 > the hungarian pastry shop

shop

s55 > swing: a concept shop

note: all maps face n

eat

e12 > café sabarsky
e18 > dovetail
e32 > lexington candy shop

note: all maps face north

manhattan:
- **midtown**
- **murray hill**
- **gramercy park**

eat

e1 > 2nd avenue deli
e13 > cho dang gol
e24 > hallo berlin
e30 > kalustyan's
e54 > the breslin
e64 > xie xie

shop

s3 > art brown international pen shop
s12 > capitol fishing tackle
s15 > complete traveller antiquarian bookstore
s25> hyman hendler & sons

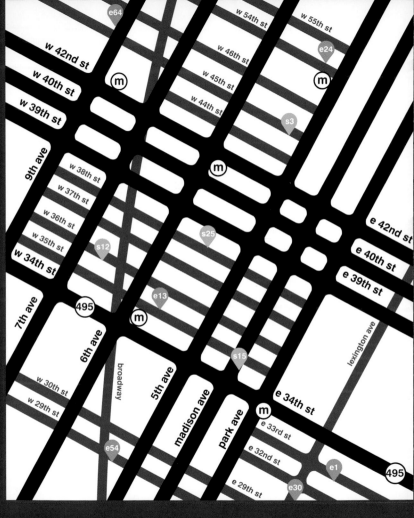

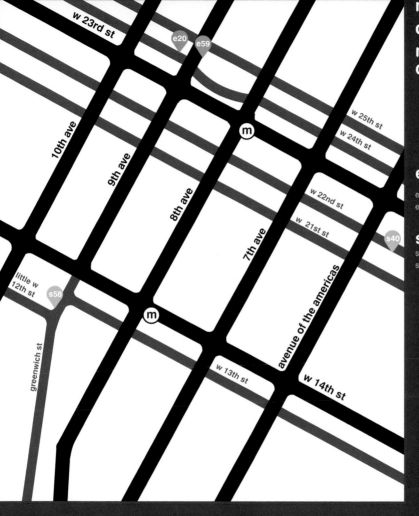

eat

e20 > el quinto pino
e59 > txikito

shop

s40 > n.y. cake & baking
s58 > the crangi family project

note: all maps face north

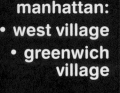

manhattan:
- ## west village
  - ## greenwich village

eat

e7 > birdbath
e23 > gottino
e27 > i sodi
e29 > joseph leonard

shop

s21 > greenwich letterpress
s32 > leffot
s62 > zero + maria cornejo

note: all maps face n

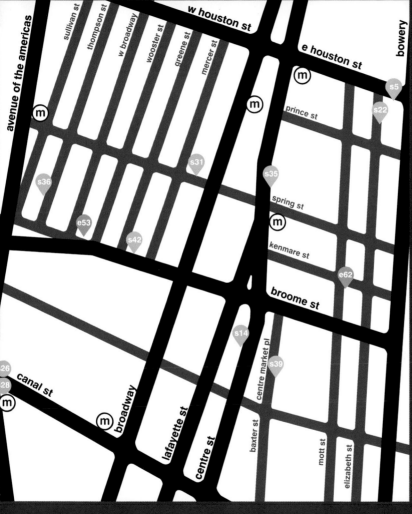

manhattan:
soho •
nolita •
little italy •

eat

e53 > sunrise mart
e62 > village tart

shop

s5 > b-4 it was cool
s14 > clic bookstore & gallery
s22 > haus interior
s26 > joanne hendricks,
cookbooks...
s28 > johnson trading gallery
s31 > kiosk
s35 > matta
s36 > meg cohen design shop
s39 > no. 6 store
s42 > ochre store

e: all maps face north

manhattan:
• east village

eat

e2 > abraço
e16 > dirt candy
e17 > double crown (off map)
e37 > mayahuel
e44 > northern spy food co.
e47 > porchetta
e57 > the redhead

shop

s13 > change of season
s27 > john derian company
(off map)
s41 > obscura antiques
and oddities
s51 < stock vintage

3rd ave
2nd ave
1st ave
ave a

east 16th st
east 15th st
east 14th st
east 13th st
east 12th st
east 11th st
east 10th st
east 9th st
saint mark's place
east 7th st
east 6th st

tompkins square park

note: all maps face n

manhattan:
lower east side (les) •
chinatown •

eat

e14 > classic coffee shop
e58 > the ten bells
e60 > vanessa's dumpling house

shop

s2 > ale et ange
s4 > assembly new york
s7 > bloodline
s9 > botanica san lazaro
s16 > dear : rivington+
s19 > fenton fallon
s34 > maryam nassir zadeh
s46 > project no. 8b
s56 > szeki
s59 > tom scott
s60 > victor osborne

all maps face north

manhattan:
• tribeca
• financial district

s38
e9
worth street
lafayette st
duane street
centre st
s44
m
greenwich st
w broadway
church st
reade street
chambers street
broadway
federal plaza
park row
pearl st
brooklyn bridge
e65
m
fulton st
beekman st
water st
s10
e4
s43
front st
fdr drive

eat

e4 > barbarini
e9 > blaue gans
e65 > zibetto

shop

s10 > bowne & co., stationers
s38 > nili lotan
43 > pasanella and son vinters
s44 > philip williams posters

note: all maps face n

notes

acorn

ultra tasteful goods for kids

323 atlantic avenue. between hoyt and smith.   a / c / g: hoyt-schermerhorn
www.acorntoyshop.com
mon - thu 11a - 6p fri - sat 11a - 7p sun noon - 6p

opened in 2004. owners: karin schaefer and diane crespo
all major credit cards accepted
online shopping. registries

boerum hill > **s01**

JH: I attribute my affinity for design and finery to the fact that it was so absent in my rural Midwest upbringing. Starved for many years of anything extraordinary, I now go to great lengths to find the unique and refined. Perhaps the owners of the wonderful children's store *Acorn* were as deprived as I because they have filled their shop with items of distinction and creativity. Better yet, these items are all for children. So never again will a child have to live with the bland and banal, that is if their parents are forward-thinking enough to shop at *Acorn*.

covet:
artemis modelling beeswax
cuquito shoes
tamar mobiles
woven play
green elf toyworks
sandy voor's leather goods
oeuf sweaters zoo
like bike

ale et ange

clothing for cool boys

40 rivington street. between forsyth and eldridge. f / v: second avenue
ale.et.ale@gmail.com
email for hours

opened in 2009. owners: osoré oyagha and eloise simonet
all major credit cards accepted

lower east side > 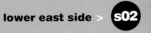 **s02**

JH: Right as this book was going to press I got word that *Ale et Ange* was moving from Chinatown to a new space on Rivington. The pictures shown here are from the original basement location that felt like a '60s era jazz musician's swinging pad. The subterranean spot was dark and moody, perfect for displaying the house designed (and made stateside) clothing that evoked the birth of cool. Maybe being underground all day finally got to owner Osoré, and he decided to pack up and head for the light. So who knows if the new *A et A* will look anything like the olds, but it will undoubtedly be cool.

covet:
ale et ange:
  button downs
  tweed for both sexes
  gingham shirts
  boxers
  t's
  belts
  loafers

art brown international pen shop

pens, pens and more pens
2 west 45th street. between fifth and sixth
b / d / f / v: 42nd street > 7: fifth avenue
212.575.5555 www.artbrown.com
mon - fri 9a - 6:30p sat 10a - 6p

opened in 1924. owner: b. warren
all major credit cards accepted
online shopping. custom orders / design

midtown westside > **s03**

JFD: I've never understood foot fetishists, but I know that if you go to Ebay and type in "used socks," you'll see undeniable evidence of this peccadillo. Now, pen fetishists I get. I am one. At *Art Brown*, I was amongst my people. You can recognize us by the glint in our eyes as we caress the lovely barrels and nibs. You can see the longing motions we make toward a stand of brilliant inks. And while the products are international, made by craftsmen hailing from Japan to Germany, so is the clientele, who have made the pilgrimage to visit this temple of writing instruments.

covet:
namiki / pilot pens
waterman pens
sailor pens
yoropen
pelikan pencils
de atramentis scented inks
diamine old english inks
moleskin city guides

assembly new york

just about perfect men's and women's boutique

174 ludlow street. between houston and stanton. f / v: second avenue
212.253.5393 www.assemblynewyork.com
daily noon - 9p

opened in 2008. owner: greg armas
all major credit cards accepted
online shopping. custom orders

lower east side > **s04**

KW: This is a town where you need to affect a certain level of blasé. Acting overly enthusiastic might get you banned to the outer boroughs or sent packing on the first flight to happy bubbly land. I've had many years to practice this disconnected nonchalance and can bring it with the best of them. But often I don't care if I'm being cool, and I actually—gasp—show that I like something or someplace. For example, *Assembly New York*. I liked just about every damn piece of extremely wearable, yet super modern clothing here and had no problems saying so. In fact I liked the boots above so much, they are now mine.

covet:
assembly collection
henrik vibskov
risto bimbiloski
a detacher
stine goya
chronicles of never
arielle de pinto
lgr glasses

b-4 it was cool

industrial antiques

89 east houston. corner of bowery
f / v: second avenue > b / d / f / v: broadway-lafayette
212.219.0139 www.b4itwascool.com
daily noon - 7p

opened in 1986. owner: gadi gilan
all major credit cards accepted

lower east side > **s05**

KW: I know there's been a downturn in this city, like everywhere else in the world, but I sincerely doubt that Gadi has felt it at his seminal industrial antiques outpost, *B-4 It Was Cool*. The reason? Because the *a la mode* style in restaurant and retail design—not just in NYC but across the country—is early Americana. Fixturing that speaks of the first 40 years or so of last century is sooooo of this century, and Gadi has stockpiles of it. Though lighting is the star here, there's also a plethora of stools, fans and some other ephemera thrown in for good measure. If you need a loan, ask Gadi for one.

covet:
vintage:
   dental lights
   toldeo stools
   american industrial lights
   holophane lights
   zafire fan
   bakelite ribbon fan
   tadpole model

baxter & liebchen

mid-century modern furnishings

33 jay street. corner of plymouth. f: york street
718.797.0630 www.baxterliebchen.com
tue - sat 10a - 6p sun noon - 6p

opened in 2005. owner: andrew kevelson
all major credit cards accepted

dumbo > s06

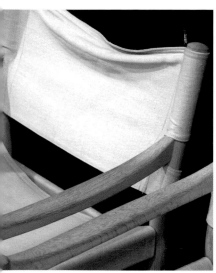

AB: Furniture styles burn bright then fade, and new trends replace old trends in the blink of an eye. To some, the rage for mid-century modern has come and gone. I, however, will always be drawn to the clean lines of this era of design, and that's why *Baxter & Liebchen* had me swooning at hello. The collection here is vast and truly impressive and no matter where you stand on trendiness or timelessness of furniture and design, you just can't argue the beauty of these pieces. Whether you've decided to embrace lacquered baroque or ethnic eclectic, you'll still desire what you can find here.

covet:
arne vodder rosewood sideboard
teak cocktail table with 3-part legs
teak & cognac leather chairs
arne vodder rosewood planter
paul henningsen white ph5 hanging lamp
arne jacobsen cylinda large coffee pot
hans wegner wishbone chairs
poul volther oak daybed

bloodline

objects for the home and life

100a forsyth steet. between grand and broome. b / d / j / f: grand street
212.533.4243 www.bloodlinenyc.blogspot.com
wed - sat noon - 7p sun noon - 6p

opened in 2008. owners: marie roldan and peggy usamanont
all major credit cards accepted
online shopping

lower east side > **s07**

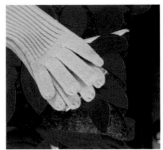

JH: Wouldn't it be cool if you could go to a super stylish friend's house and be able to buy all of his or her furnishings and knick-knacks and transfer them all to your house so you could seem like the design savant? Unfortunately, "I love that lamp—how much will you take for it?" is inappropriate cocktail conversation. Shopping at *Bloodline* is as close as you're going to get to this fantasy. Outfitted like an apartment, with objects for the home and self, the hand-chosen selection here is personal and eclectic. And Marie is so nice, you'll likely invite her over to show off your new *Bloodline* bounty.

covet:
yarnz cashmere gloves
etched botanical glasses
vintage piggy bank
vintage irish linen towels
drew morrison printer block table
drew morrison flask lamp
alexander ferguson pillows
aigle boots

173

blueberi

women's clothing and jewelry

143 front street. between pearl and jay. f: york street
718.422.7724 www.beristores.com
tue - sat 11a - 8p sun 11a - 7p

opened in 2006. owner: suewayne brown
all major credit cards accepted
online shopping

dumbo > s08

AB: I am lucky to have had not just one, but two, grandmothers with a serious flair for unusual jewelry. When I was a child I loved playing wlth their respective jewelry boxes which consisted of costume jewelry, pieces from their far-flung travels, artist-made baubles and more. At *Blueberi*, I felt like my grandmothers eclectic jewelry boxes came to life. Suewayne designs most of the jewelry here herself, and she pairs each intriguing piece with the equally intriguing clothing. Being at *Blueberi* was as much fun as being ten again, except now I'm truly able to dress up, not just play at it.

covet:
blueberi jewelry
vivienne westwood coat
sonia jacket
mason
frye boots
abigail glaum-lathbury coat
twinkle by wenlan
adore leggings

175

botanica san lazaro

not just for santeria anymore
127 rivington street. between essex and norfolk. f / j / m / z: essex street-delancey
212.529.4747
daily 10a - 5p

opened in 1987. owner: efrain diaz
cash only

lower east side > **s09**

KW: I am not a practitioner of Santeria. In fact, I'm stone cold petrified of anything voodooesque. Maybe I watched *Angel Heart* one too many times. So it might seem a bit daft that I love botanicas like *Botanica San Lazaro*, which you could also think of as a Santeria superstore. I love these places not because I'm planning to do any hexing in the future, but because they are great spots to get candles and also perfumes and home sprays which offer life assistance like the "jackpot" spray. Though I spritz this daily throughout my house and studio, I am waiting for the voodoo to work.

covet:
jinx remover
crucifixes
salvadera aromatic plant bath
dominating perfume
florida water cologne
ray chia collection "ñino jesus"
candles

bowne & co., stationers

historical letterpress stationer and gift shop
211 water street. between fulton and beekman
2 / 3 / 4 / 5 / j / z / m: fulton street > a / c: broadway-nassau
212.748.8651 www.southstreetseaportmuseum.org
daily 10a - 6p

opened in 1775. master printer and curator: robert warner
all major credit cards accepted
classes

financial district >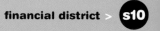

CD: I have a tiny addiction to paper stores. But I'm tired of twee and dainty paperies. I want the hard stuff. I want to see letterpresses and smell the ink. I want to feel like I'm walking through someone's attic, finding boxes of fonts and textures. Thanks to *Bowne & Co.'s* master printer Robert, I've finally found it. Maybe the fact that this business (originally in a different location) has been printing since 1775 helps create its mystique. Or maybe it's just the haphazard displays of both clever and obscure paper art that make this shop feel like a fascinating figment of one person's papery mind.

covet:
bowne & co. walt whitman cards
hand-stitched onion paper journals
box set of woodcut cards
vintage french metal threads
moleskin notebook covered in vintage paper
hand letterpressed brookfield notes
punch out paper animal figurines

brook farm general store

tasteful, useful stuff

75 south sixth street. between berry and wyeth
j / m / z: marcy avenue > l: bedford avenue
718.388.8642 www.brookfarmgeneralstore.com
mon, tue - sun noon - 8p sun 1 - 6p

opened in 2009. owners: philippa content and christopher winterbourne
visa. mc
online shopping

williamsburg > **s11**

KW: Though I like to think of myself as a kind and benevolent boss, I think the *eat.shop* authors might describe me a little less kindly. Like Jon, whom I made tromp through a massive spring snowstorm to take a picture of a steak at *Prime Meats* and then traverse back to Williamsburg to visit *Brook Farm* (if you read about somebody being mugged for his or her cross-country skis during this time, Jon was for sure the attacker). Though the journey here inspired a plentitude of !@!#, the experience at *Brook Farm* was nothing less than magical. A worthwhile place in which to journey.

covet:
tourne chun mee green tea
fog linen works leather key holders
andlepoise desk light
stanley flasks
elementary screwdriver sets
sigg metal lunchboxes
vintage 1930s money clip
japanese scrub brushes

capitol fishing tackle

the oldest tackle shop in new york

132 west 36th street. between seventh and broadway. 1 / 2 / 3: 34th street
212.929.6132 www.capitolfishing.com
see website for hours

opened in 1897. owner: richie collins
visa. mc

midtown westside > **s12**

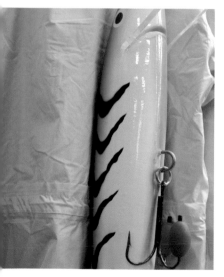

JH: I don't know why anything in New York would surprise me, yet *Capitol Fishing Tackle* does. I expected a slick, high tech boutique of a store—a place where Gordon Gekko might go to buy a $1,000 reel for a one-time fishing "meeting" in Patagonia. Instead I found a fishing store where salty old men stood around discussing knots and where there's never been a merchandiser on staff. It would be easy to find a place like this in Astoria, OR, or Mystic, CT, but within casting distance of Times Square? Improbable. Call me naive, but I am charmed by its honest-to-goodness authenticity.

covet:
martinez bamboo fly rod
against the elements rain gear
fenwick poles
okuma reels
gooey bobs
ugly stik
berus boots
lead sinkers

183

change of season

hand-picked past-season gems

341 east ninth street. between first and second avenues
l: first avenue > 6: astor place
212.420.7770 www.changeofseasonnyc.com
tue - thu 1 - 7:30p fri - sun noon - 8p

opened in 2009. owners: clinton curtis and marco querci
all major credit cards accepted

east village > **s13**

KW: I used to imagine that I would be a fashion photographer. The closest I got was when I shot my roommate and her friend, styled with layers of pearls and lace gloves *à la* Madonna in her "Like a Virgin" era. After this fleeting stab at photographic glory, I decided others were better suited for this gig. I didn't lose my love of the craft though and have avidly collected photography books ever since—starting with Bruce Weber's *O Rio de Janiero*. *Clic Bookstore* is therefore like photonip to me. If I could, I would transfer the entire store to my own personal library.

covet:
guy bourdin
david lachapelle
araki
julie blackmon
matthew rolston
malick sidibe
peter beard
helmut newton

complete traveller
antiquarian bookstore

vintage travel books and maps

199 madison avenue. corner of 35th. 6: 33rd street
212.685.9007 www.ctrarebooks.com
mon - fri 9:30a - 6:30p sat 10a - 6p sun noon - 5p

opened in 1978. owner: arnie greenberg
all major credit cards accepted
online shopping

murray hill / gramercy park > s15

KW: What do I do for a living? I'm the publisher of a series of travel guides. So you would think I might have a deep knowledge of the history of this publishing genre. Insert sound of gong here. Sadly, I had never seen a Baedeker guide until I entered the *Complete Traveller*. Just so you don't think I'm a complete numbskull, I do collect other guides from all over the world, but none more than about 15 years old. Here there are guides, travel writings and maps that were published toward the beginning of the 20th century. This is what you call having a good shelf life.

covet:
wpa american guides
baedeker guides
panorama guides
tibet & nepal by a. henry savage landor
le tour du monde en velocipede
argosy magazine
vintage maps
great selection of nyc books

dear : rivington +

wearable avant garde and curated pieces for home

95 rivington street. between ludlow and orchard. f / j / m / z: essex street-delancey
212.673.3494 www.dearrivington.com
daily noon - 8p

opened in 2009. owners: moon rhee and heyja do
all major credit cards accepted
custom orders / design

lower east side > **s16**

KW: I worked in retail in NYC during in the '80s. My first gig was at Kansai Yamamoto where I sold cartoonish asymmetrical, appliquéd sweaters and cartoonesque designs. Then I worked at Charivari Workshop and most all my dosh was spent on acquiring Comme des Garçons, Yohji Yamamoto and Matsuda pieces. I admit, I still have a soft spot for that early era of Japanese clothing design and I felt its essence in full force at *Dear : Rivington+*. Yes ladies, you can wear a parachute pant if it's designed by Heyja. And if you lust after the original pieces, the stock of vintage Japanese design here is excellent.

covet:
dear:
  clothing
  shoes & accessories
vintage:
  martin margiela
  yohji yamamoto
  issey miyake
  upstairs dedicated to vintage furniture, etc.

191

erie basin

eclectic antiques, furniture, jewelry and folk art

388 van brunt street. between dikeman and coffey. bus: 61 / 77
718.554.6147 www.eriebasin.com tw: @eriebasin
thu - sat noon - 7p sun noon - 6p

opened in 2006. owner: russell whitmore
all major credit cards accepted
online shopping

red hook >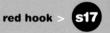

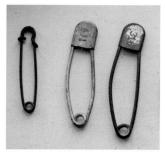

CD: I wish I had bought that white porcelain wing I saw at *Erie Basin*. I'd made the stupid assumption that there were other stores like it that would have other wings like that, but I haven't found anything remotely similar since. Why? That's because *Erie Basin* is like no other store. Many of the pieces here are one-of-a kind, whether antique or contemporary. Russell picks each piece—be it an Edwardian glove box or an Etruscan revival bracelet—with a poetic eye, and his finds often tell a winsome secret or a long-forgotten story. Unfortunately the story of that porcelain wing is that it's not mine.

covet:
masonic carved wall shelf
giant victorian hair comb
empire mahogany recamier
early 1800s portait of mary on ivory
steel & mother of pearl souvenir purse
edwardian ivory heart belt
conroy+wilcox rose cut black diamond ring
lee hale thorn studs

eva gentry

sharp, urban, high-end women's fashion

389 atlantic avenue. between hoyt and bond. a / c / g / 2 / 3: hoyt-schermerhorn
718.260.9033 www.evagentry.com
mon - sat 11a - 7p sun 11a - 6p

opened in 2009. owners: eva and gentry dayton
all major credit cards accepted

boerum hill > **s18**

JH: You could easily say *Eva Gentry* offers the best selection of high-end women's designer clothing in Brooklyn. They sell lines rarely seen on the east side of the Brooklyn Bridge. But calling out Brooklyn somehow diminishes the excellence of this shop. It's akin to an award for Best in Show for dogs with white fur only. *Eva Gentry* has great clothing, and it happens to be located in Brooklyn. But there is more. In fact, just next door is their consignment store which offers the same level of sharp, smart fashion but with more affordable price tags. A ha! A leg up.

covet:
dries van noten
jas m.b.
maison martin margiela
rick owens
guidi
michelle fantaci
harputs
cire trudon

fenton fallon

'80s fabulous jewelry and vintage clothing

end of freeman alley. just off chrystie. j / m: bowery
212.477.1315 www.danalorenz.com tw: @danalorenz
tue - sat noon - 7p

opened in 2009. owner: dana lorenz
all major credit cards accepted

lower east side > **s19**

KW: Without doing a lick of research, I'm going to take a stab in the dark and guess that Dana named her jewelry line after Fallon Carrington, the naughty minx on *Dynasty*. And Fenton? Maybe he was the butler on the show, who knows. But let's get back to the 21st century and the real story. Dana's first line was *Fenton* which is very Alexis Carrington, in both price and style. Next came *Fallon* which, like its imagined namesake, is younger and sassier and has a lighter price tag. The two lines commingle at this space the size of Krystle Carrington's boudoir.

covet:
dome stone cuff
wild at heart earrings
hoffs bracelet
cairo chandelier earrings
infinity segmented necklace
isis cuff
christiane earrings
spikes & crystals bangles

foxy & winston

whimsical screen-printed clothes and paperie

392 van brunt street. between dikeman and coffey. bus: 61 / 77
718.928.4855 www.foxyandwinston.com tw: @foxyandwinston
mon - tue appointment only wed - sun noon - 6p

opened in 2009. owner: jane buck
all major credit cards accepted
online shopping. custom orders / design

red hook > s20

CD: It's no mistake that there are six Red Hook establishments featured in this book, though it's surprising considering this area was barely on anyone's radar ten years ago. Just about every establishment in this neighborhood embodies a certain "living-the-artist's-dream" ethos. And *Foxy & Winston* is no exception. Jane hand prints all her own cards, canvasses and kids' clothes in the back of her store. Her artistic contentedness comes through in the bright, happy hues. If I was a part of this community, I suspect I'd feel like I was living the dream also.

covet:
foxy & winston:
  organic cotton lovebug bibs
  pig drinking from teacup greeting card
  baby owl t's
  hand-printed muslin bags
  golden hamster onesie
  framed & matted limited hedgehog print
  hand-printed gift boxes

greenwich letterpress

letterpress card shop

39 christopher street. between waverly and west tenth. 1: christopher street
212.989.7464 www.greenwichletterpress.com tw: @greenwichletterpress
tue - fri 11a - 7p sat - sun noon - 6p

opened in 2006. owners: beth salvini and amy salvini-swanson
all major credit cards accepted
online shopping. custom orders / design

greenwich village > **s21**

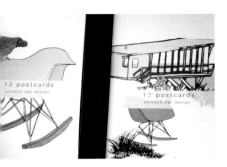

AB: I just started taking a letterpress class, which has more than doubled my already high and glowing view of the craft. Metal typefaces, hand-setting type, learning the tricks and techniques of how to lay out and print—all of this strikes me as I look at the beautiful cards and paper products on display at *Greenwich Letterpress*. While I am excited to say I just hand-set my first line of type, spelling out my name in proud Copperplate Bold, I don't plan on giving up my paper store obsession anytime soon. *Greenwich Letterpress* is a habit I have no desire to break.

covet:
custom greenwich letterpress products
nikki mcclure things to make & do
enormous champion letterpress whale cards
la famiglia green cards
austin press
crayon rocks
yee-haw industries
egg press

haus interior

an interior designer's home shop

250 elizabeth street. between houston and prince
f / v: second avenue > b / d / f / v: broadway-lafayette
212.741.0455 www.hausinterior.com tw: @hausinterior
mon - sat 11a - 7p sun noon - 6p

opened in 2009. owner: nina v. freudenberger
all major credit cards accepted
online shopping. design services

nolita >

AB: Television is chock-a-block with the scourge of reality programming, which includes shows featuring everyday people who imagine themselves interior designers. And though these shows make it seem like someone with no experience could miraculously transform into a gifted designer overnight, this is nothing more than good old-fashioned fantasy. If you want the real deal, visit Nina at *Haus Interior*. Not only will you be influenced by her fresh design vision, but you can walk out of here with pieces that work with your bank balance. Good design does come at a price: affordable.

covet:
seagrass cubes
fog linen napkins
vintage navy award pillows
brass trophy lamp
brushstroke plate
roost glass canteen
letterpress bookplates
vintage trunk

203

hollander & lexer

wearable fashions for men

358 atlantic avenue. between hoyt and bond. a / c / g / 2: hoyt-schermerhorn
103 metropolitan avenue. corner of wythe. l: bedford > g: metropolitan
718.797.9190 / 718.797.9117 www.hollanderandlexer.net
see website for hours

opened in 2006. owners: hicham benmira and brian cousins
visa. mc

boerum hill / williamsburg > **s23**

JH: Sometimes I look at men's fashion shows on Style.com and roll my eyes. I mean, really, what man is going to wear patent leather hot pants with a bat-wing, animal-print cardigan on top? It's entertaining but has nothing to do with the real world—unlike *Hollander & Lexer*, whose selection of labels and house brand are totally wearable and still fashionable. Not to mention that the store has an antique repair-shop meets industrial-shipyard kind of feeling. What could get more masculine than that? Believe me, it helps you feel butch when you sniff the Santa Maria Novella bath salts.

covet:
hollander & lexer wool pants
barbour
alexander yamaguchi henleys
c.p. company
khadi + co. scarves
drakes knit tie
chronicles of never glasses
darr: h & l's sibling store

holler & squall

antiques and furnishings

71 atlantic avenue. corner of hicks. 4 / 5: borough hall
347.405.3734 hollerandsquall.blogspot.com
thu - fri noon - 7p sat - sun 11a - 7p

opened in 2009. owners: zachariah and gillette wing
all major credit cards accepted
custom orders

boerum hill >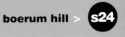

JH: You would think my house would be exquisitely outfitted with the amount of shopping I am required to do for this job. It should be, but it isn't. Call it the cobbler's kid syndrome (i.e., the kid going barefoot). To get it up to snuff, I should buy a few of the goodies at *Holler & Squall* and my humble abode would be nearly camera ready. The selection of carefully culled antiques and oddities are just what's needed to perk up my Ikea-centric living quarters. My problem now is deciding what to buy, and I'm going to kick myself if I make the wrong decision. Better buy it all.

covet:
wooden cigar molds
bone alligator
hand-carved wooden race horse
wooden hat forms
candle snuffer / wick cutters
wooden airplane
custom reclaimed wooden shelves
old metal card catalog

hyman hendler & sons

third generation ribbon store

21 west 38th street. between 5th and 6th. b / d / f / v: bryant park
212.840.8393 www.hymanhendler.com
mon - fri 9a - 5p

opened in 1900. owner: michael weisman
all major credit cards accepted

midtown westside > **s25**

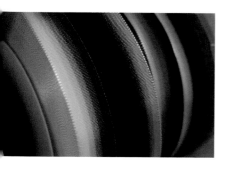

JH: Ribbon stores seem like something out of the past. Their heyday evokes a time when people either made their own clothes or needed an adornment to perk up a droopy mood. This notion seems positively Depression era, so how can a ribbon store make it today? Hmmm. What's old is new again? What goes around comes around? I certainly see a lot of droopy moods needing a little pick-me-up. *Hyman Hendler* is a ribbon wonderland that's seen good times and bad times—always focusing on supplying incredible ribbon. And without a government bailout either.

covet:
mackintosh scarves
velvet ribbon
ultra-wide grosgrains
vintage jacquards
luxurious 76 satins
royalty picot taffeta
wire edged velvet stripes
velvet plaids

joanne hendricks, cookbooks...

vintage cookbooks and more

488 greenwich street. between canal and spring. 1: canal street
212.226.5731 www.joannehendrickscookbooks.com
daily 11:30a - 7p (call before you come)

opened in 1995. owner: joanne hendricks
all major credit cards accepted
online shopping

soho >

KW: I am married to a really good cook. But he doesn't use cookbooks. He's the master of a little of this, a dash of that—*et voila*, coq au vin! I, on the other hand, am a bit challenged in the culinary arts. When I use his methodology, I get soup cookies. So cookbooks are my friends. Especially vintage ones with beautiful illustrations, and *Joanne Hendricks* has a stunning collection. This tucked-away nook of a bookstore in a federal-style rowhouse is around the corner from the legendary *Ear Inn* where you can take your just-bought copy of *Toasts You Ought To Know* to impress your bar mates.

covet:
bocca series of cookbooks
the gastronomical me by m.f.k. fisher
jane grigson's vegetable book by jane grigson
the tyrolese cookery book by david de bethel
hu-kwa tea
vintage menus
wedgewood teapot
swid powell zurich service

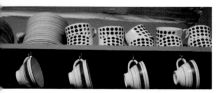

john derian company

glorious decoupage and more

6 east second street. between bowery and second. f / v: second avenue
212.677.3917 www.johnderian.com
tue - sun noon - 7p

opened in 1989. owner: john derian
all major credit cards accepted

east village >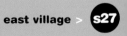

AB: *John Derian* might be well on his way to taking over the world, which I personally think would be pretty great. I am constantly coming across his decoupage designs in stores across the country while I *eat.shop*. I can almost always guarantee the place is good if *John Derian* is sold at an establishment. Nothing though compares to the experience of John's own store, which is a world of wonderful and beyond. If you haven't been here before, you are missing out on an extraordinary retail experience. It's one of my favorite places in this city.

covet:
john derian:
  decoupage plates & platters
  paperweights
artemas quibble leather bracelets
hugo guiness prints
astier de villatte candles
feather dusters
beekman pure goat milk soap

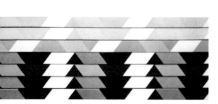

johnson trading gallery

collectible furniture

490 greenwich street. between canal and spring. 1: canal street
212.925.1110 www.johnsontradinggallery.com
mon - fri 11a - 7p sat noon - 6p

opened in 2002. owner: paul johnson
all major credit cards accepted
online shopping (first dibs)

soho > **s28**

KW: As I was leaving *Joanne Hendricks*, the October rain kicked into a full downpour and I put my umbrella in horizontal shield position. A couple of doors down I chanced being permanently blinded by rain daggers to take a peek in the window of *Johnson Trading Gallery*. What caught my attention was the Kwangho Lee "knitted" sofa made of black rubber tubing. I needed to see some more, come hell or high water. Inside was what I had been scouring the city for: unusual, artful, collectible, contemporary furniture. If you believe that furnishings can double as artistic statements, *JTG* will delight.

covel:
max lamb
joseph heidecker
ben jones
kwangho lee
aranda / lasch
mario dal fabbro
simon hasan
greg lynn

jumelle

nicely edited collection of women's clothing

148 bedford avenue. between eighth and ninth. l: bedford avenue
718.388.9525 www.shopjumelle.com
mon 1 - 7:30p tue - sat noon - 7:30p sun noon - 7p

opened in 2006. owner: candice waldron
all major credit cards accepted
online shopping

williamsburg > 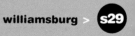 **s29**

JFD: Little girls are warned by cluckish parents not to wear patent-leather shoes because little boys might get a peek up their skirts in the reflection. Big girls therefore, rush out to buy patent leather shoes. At least that's what I did. *Jumelle* had a perfect pair of patent loafers—a little pointy, very suave and polished to a blinding sheen. They would have paired perfectly with some of the equally enticing clothes that Candice selectively brings in. Modesty be damned—while I'm at it, I also want that Alexander Wang zipper-fronted dress. Let's see what the little boys make of that.

covet:
karen walker
isabel marant
bodkin
hope
mociun
aesa
gaspard yurkievich
swedish hasbeens

kill devil hill

fine goods of all descriptions
170 franklin street. between kent and java. g: greenpoint avenue
347.534.3088
thu - tue noon - 8p

opened in 2008. owners: mark straiton and mary brockman
all major credit cards accepted
custom orders

greenpoint > **s30**

JH: I could never own a shop like *Kill Devil Hill*. Don't get me wrong—the shop's honky-tonk meets Appalachian backwoods antiques and objects are great. But If this was my place, I wouldn't be able to let go of anything. I would constantly second guess myself, convinced that *The Golden Girls* 20th anniversary plate should be priced extremely high due to its brilliance and popularity. As illustrated, I shouldn't be in retail. I'll leave it to those who have excellent taste like Mark and Mary, and I'll stick to watching the *GG*s fight over the last piece of cheesecake.

covet:
b.s. mercantile cravats
b.s. mercantile custom pants
taxidermy beaver
antlers by the pound
brooklyn brine pickles
vintage coffee / tea kitten
vintage '30s chambray shirt

kiosk

eclectic finds from all over the world

95 spring street, second floor. between mercer and broadway
r / w: prince street > 6: spring street
212.226.8601 www.kioskkiosk.com
tue - sat noon - 7p

opened in 2005. owner: alisa grifo
visa. mc
online shopping

soho > **s31**

AB: NYC has always been a place where retail risk-takers abound. But then came the downturn, and some of these visionaries went by the wayside. So what's left is a number of hardy survivors, and playing it safe seems a reasonable thing to do. So who's still pushing the envelope? *Kiosk*. This always has been and remains a one-of-a-kind retail experience where carefully curated items are culled from Alisa's adventures abroad. Mini-exhibitions are constantly in rotation. At last check, the Groundhog's Day theme was happening. Need some nut creme from Sweden?

covet:
horsehair hand broom & red metal dustpan
natural disk rattle
lavender oil from provence
danish dishbrush
encerite wax from portugal
horn haircombs
fennia marking pen
red dot tengui

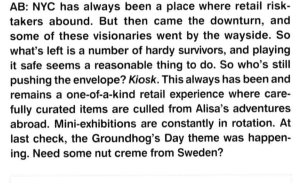

leffot

exquisitely crafted men's shoes

10 christopher street. between waverly and greenwich
1: christopher street > all lines: west fourth street
212.989.4577 www.leffot.com tw: @leffot
mon - sat 11a - 7p sun noon - 6p

opened in 2008. owner: steven taffel
all major credit cards accepted

greenwich village > **s32**

AB: My grandfather's shoe size is 15. My grandmother wore a size 8. When they traveled the world, she packed her shoes inside of his, to protect them and save space. To this day, when I see gorgeously made men's shoes, I can't help but think of my grandmother nestling her elegant Ferragamos inside my grandfather's battleships. He would have been well served by some of the exquisitely crafted shoes found at *Leffot*. And now that they carry a small selection of women's shoes also, I can imagine what my grandmother would have chosen. Or even better, what I will choose.

covet:
shoes:
  church
  gaziano
  edward green
  alden
  made-to-order pairs
ephtee trunks handmade in france
polishing leather map

le grenier

vintage goods, emphasis on good

19 greenpoint avenue. between west street and transmitter park

g: greenpoint avenue

718.569.0111 www.legrenierny.com

wed - thu 1 - 8p fri - sat noon - 8p sun noon - 7p

opened in 2009. owner: maya marzolf

all major credit cards accepted

greenpoint > **s33**

JH: Everything sounds better in Le French. I learned long ago that peppering my language with a well placed *mon dieu* or a *zut alors!* makes for a much better story. The lovely Maya clearly learned this lesson by naming her Greenpoint shop *Le Grenier*—French for "the attic." Think about it. "The attic" elicits visions of cast-off bread makers and worn-once Snuggies. Quite the opposite, *Le Grenier* is filled with beautiful, ornate silver table settings and fetching cafe au lait bowls. Perhaps it's just truth in advertising, but *Le Grenier* is *fantastique*.

covet:
antique mini paper cutters
circus glasses
staffordshire dishware
antique oil lamp
vintage napkins
silver place settings
etched sports glasses
vintage desk lamps

225

maryam nassir zadeh

retail storytelling

123 norfolk street. corner of rivington. f / j / m / z: essex street-delancey
212.673.6405 www.maryamnassirzadeh.com
daily noon - 8p

opened in 2008. owners: maryam nassir zadeh and uday kak
all major credit cards accepted

lower east side > 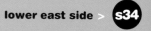 **s34**

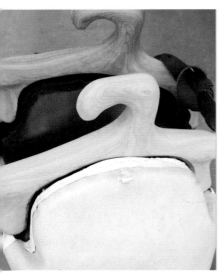

KW: Though I want to believe I'm a good storyteller, deep down I know that's a pipe dream. When I tell a story I take forever to get to the interesting part, and the poor people listening get stuck hearing a litany of "umms" and "likes." Yawn. *Maryam Nassir Zadeh* is a great storyteller, and she doesn't have to utter a word. To hear her tales, all you need to do is walk in the door of her eponymous retail world. Walking through here is like turning the pages of a Gabriel Garcia Marquez novel. Each vignette of beautifully sourced clothing and accessories is positioned to make you ponder, and then acquire.

covet:
lindsey thornburg
eatable of many orders
ohne titel
confetti system
creatures of the wind
jeremy laing
haltbar
jensen-conroy

matta

globally inspired clothing, accessories and home décor

241 lafayette street. between prince and spring. 6: spring street
212.343.9399 www.mattany.com
daily 11:30a - 7p

opened in 2005. owner: cristina gitti
all major credit cards accepted
online shopping

nolita > **s35**

AB: My friend Anne is one of those women who could wear a paper bag and still look chic. This has to do with her innate sense of style and most importantly her way with accessories. When we were wandering around No-lita together, we aimed toward *Matta* and their beautiful ethnic-inspired wares. Anne loves the metallic totes here and I, following my own inner accessorizing voice, was drawn to the tunics and the dupatta scarves with their tasseled ends. After shopping here, even the most accessory-challenged will feel more confident in their ability to wear a paper bag and look great.

covet:
matta:
   silk & cotton tunics & dresses
   dupatta scarf
   dhurri rug
   rajastani blanket
   metallic tote bag
   india: the matta coloring book
   maya bracelets

meg cohen design shop

luxe cashmere accessories

59 thompson street. between spring and broome. c / e: spring street
212.966.3733 www.megcohendesign.com
mon - sat 11a - 7p sun 11a - 6p

opened in 2006. owner: meg cohen
all major credit cards accepted
online shopping

soho > **s36**

AB: When it comes to keeping warm during the dregs of winter (and this one has been a doozy), style often gets thrown out the window. But my new friend *Meg Cohen* has solved this quandary for me with her gorgeous knits. Before you could say "abominable snowman," I had snapped up a cashmere head scarf and fingerless mittens. There were a number of other treasures and curiosities that appealed and were calling my name, but I decided to ignore the siren's call, knowing that I would be back in spring to stock up for the warm months.

covet:
meg cohen:
  scarves
  hats
  gloves
  serapes
  cashmere blanket
vintage cuff links
vintage charm necklaces

metal & thread

local artisan shop and found-object gallery

398 van brunt street. between coffey and dikeman streets. bus: 61 / 77
718.414.9651 www.metalthread.com
mon, wed - sun noon - 6p

opened in 2008. owners: denise carbonell and derek dominy
all major credit cards accepted
online shopping

red hook >  **s37**

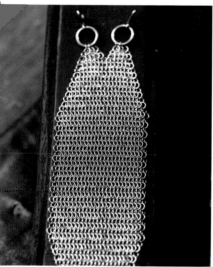

CD: If there was ever a shop that represented the definition of handmade, it's *Metal & Thread*. Co-owner Derek welded all the steel shelves in the store and forged most of the jewelry on display, from steel mesh earrings to a chain-mail necklace. In contrast to his metal creations are the much softer works of art by co-owner, Denise. Interspersed with their handmade goods are plenty of found objects and salvaged industrial scraps that couple as art. No matter how much moola you have in your pocket, you'll walk out with something that's assuredly one-of-a-kind.

covet:
handmade stainless-steel mesh neck wrap
charles flickinger slump glass bowl
lemon citrine teardrop necklace
old, crusty pocket knife with leather pouch
denise carbonell painted hands
horn & black glass bead necklace
1930s sterling silver handmade mexican lariat
italian coral drop earrings

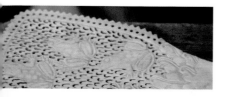

nili lotan

downtown minimalism for women

188 duane street. corner of greenwich street. 1 / 2 / 3: chambers street
212.219.8794 www.nililotan.com tw: @nililotan
daily mon - sun noon - 7p

opened in 2003. owner: nili lotan
all major credit cards accepted

tribeca >

KW: New York City is filled with all sort of female urban breeds. There's the Upper East Siders with their sharp bobs, sharper heels and scarily perfect tailoring. Then there's the Brooklynites, who are often accompanied by their bearded mate and sometimes a cub. Then there are the Downtowners. They stay below 14th, wouldn't get caught with a spray tan and embrace fashion individuality. All three of these breeds could and would wear *Nili Lotan*. Her clothing is the essence of modern simplicity—classic and yet supremely urban. She's a best of her breed.

covet:
nili lotan:
   rosalie dress
   brian stripe halter top
   elio jacket
   sequined emma top
   willa dress
   perfect white jean
   skinny leather pants

no. 6 store

contemporary and vintage women's clothing

6 centre market place. between broome and grand. 6: spring street
212.226.5759 www.no6store.com tw: @no6store
mon - sat noon - 7p sun noon - 6p

opened in 2005. owners: morgan yakus and karin bereson
all major credit cards accepted

little italy > **s39**

AB: The first time I visited *No. 6*, I felt like I was walking into a party of good friends at someone's house. Ladies were lounging on the couch, giving advice to each other while trying on various pieces. One of the owners was pulling clothing like she was grabbing items from her own closet. I could have felt like an outsider intruding, but the exact opposite was true. The vibe here is nothing but warm and friendly which makes you want to sit down and pull on a pair of *No. 6*'s of-the-moment clog boots or slip into one of the sweet vintage-inspired dresses. If you still find me here next month, don't be surprised.

covet:
no. 6:
  light woodland floral silk print dress
  black velvet & lace overlap dress
  leather buckle clog boot
  aviator leather shearling clog boot
wendy nichol bags
arielle de pinto web necklace
aesa ancient tongues necklace

n.y. cake & baking

a baker's disneyland

56 west 22nd street. between fifth and sixth avenues. f / v: 23rd street
212.675.cake www.nycake.com
mon - sat 10a - 6p

opened in 1985. owner: joan mansour
all major credit cards accepted
online shopping. classes

chelsea >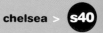

JFD: I've been making complicated special-occasion cakes for almost a decade now, not professionally, but well enough that when friends require a cake, they know they can turn to me. Over this time I've had dozens of disasters: cakes that list, frostings that melt, ganaches that leak. Yet what I love most about cakes is how forgiving they are. Pile on more frosting! Cover with sprinkles! No surprise then that when I entered the vast and wondrous *N.Y. Cake & Baking*, I didn't see just the promise of future cakes—I saw the promise of future cake fixes. There's everything you need here and more.

covet:
chocolate molds
cake pans in all sizes & shapes
impression mats
food colorings, sugars & sprinkles
pastry tips
edible sugar gems
cupcake sleeves & wrappers
petal, luster & disco dusts

obscura antiques & oddities

fun, weird things

280 east tenth street. between first and a. l: first avenue > 6: astor place
212.505.9251 www.obscuraantiques.com
mon - sun noon - 8p

opened in 1991. owners: mike zohn and evan michaelson
all major credit cards accepted

east village >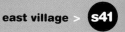

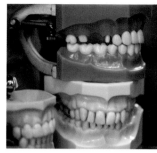

JFD: How's this for a cross-section of society? When I asked *Obscura Antique's* owner Mike what kind of customer regularly frequents his store, he offered: movie people, fetishists and corporate types (with Jon Peters, you get three in one). Movie types I can see: props are needed when filming flicks like *Seven* or *Saw*. Fetishists: the masks, capes and medical oddities compute. Corporate types: I'm assuming that folks like myself fall into this category as I enjoyed scanning the shelves for antique false teeth and pickled lobster embryos. My take: The items here may be obscura, but they're also funa.

covet:
victorian taxidermy
medical oddities
freemason paraphernalia
masks
vintage photos & postcards
capes
apothecary products
ventriloquist dummies

ochre store

rustic modern housewares

462 broome street. between mercer and greene. 6: spring street
212.414.4332 www.ochrestore.com / www.canvashomestore.com
mon - sat 11a - 7p sun noon - 6p

opened in 1996. owners: joanna bibby, harriet maxwell macdonald,
solenne de la fouchardière and andrew corrie
all major credit cards accepted
online shopping

soho >

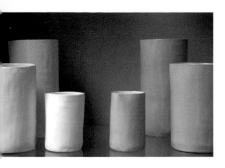

AB: Usually I like a place based on the visual aspects. But at *Ochre*, my initial love feelings came from how it smelled. Not that I've been in a country farmhouse slash urbane Argentinian mountain home, but I think that's how it would smell. As for the visuals, they are just as good here: striking furniture, minimalistic accessories like wooden planks and handwoven organic linen napkins—it's so calming—which is such a contrast to the world of traffic and steel just outside the doors. Take a scan of *Ochre's* world and know that a piece of it can be in your world also.

pasanella and son vintners

wine, spirits and drinking ephemera

115 south street. between peck slip and beekman
a / c / 2 / 3 / 4 / 5: fulton street / broadway-nassau
212.233.8383 www.pasanellaandson.com
mon - sat 10a - 9p sun noon - 7p

opened in 2006. owner: marco pasanella wine director: ryan ibsen
all major credit cards accepted
onling shopping. classes

financial district > **e43**

CD: Despite the fact that I've spent the last decade as a food and wine writer, I often dreaded editing stories about the grape. I love wine, sure, and I know a fair share of oenophilic lingo—but, frankly, wine culture was just too serious for me. If, however, Marco ruled the wine world, that would be another story. Shopping in his store, *Pasanella and Sons*, makes wine and its accoutrements fun. From bottle stoppers in the shape of a horse's head to rare Barolos to a vintage car that acts as a wine display—shopping for a bottle here pleasantly erases all traces of my serious wine writer days.

covet / imbibe:
98 pol roger cuvee winston churchill
08 burlotto verduno pelaverga
pierre gimmonet brut nv
black maple hill bourbon
marolo barolo grappa
vintage brass key corkscrew
themed baskets
vintage hand-cut floral water glasses

245

philip williams posters

largest vintage poster gallery in the world

122 chambers street (entrance on warren also). between church and west broadway
1 / 2 / 3: chambers street > a / c / e: west broadway
212.513.0313 www.postermuseum.com
mon - sat 11a - 7p

opened in 1973. owner: philip williams
all major credit cards accepted
online shopping. custom searches

tribeca >

KW: My love of posters began in 1982 when I was in Spain during the World Cup. My brother and I snatched every poster of the event that wasn't glued down. Later in the '80s I was studying in Japan, and I was given an extraordinary poster by the designer Gan Hosoya. And in the '90s I started collecting posters from *Hatch Show Print* in Nashville. But now it's a new century and I haven't bought any posters yet. That soon will be rectified at *Philip Williams*. I have no worries of finding something extraordinary here because this place is vast with a capital V, and the collection is awesome. Vive la poster!

covet:
posters:
  tourot muckens for philips
  jacques barthes' nimes
  furu's rosy rosy
  niko's new mafia boss
  milton glaser's floating pear
vintage magazines
advertising ephemera

pomme

children's shop with french style

81 washington street. between front and york. f: york street
186 duane street. between greenwich and hudson. 1 / 2 / 3: chambers
718.855.0623 www.pommenyc.com
tue - sat 11a - 7p sun 11a - 6p

opened in 2005. owners: samantha adam and stephanie chayet
all major credit cards accepted

dumbo / tribeca > **s45**

AB: The children in Paris always seem so beautifully dressed. If you spend a lazy Sunday afternoon in the Luxembourg Gardens watching the boys in their sweaters and slacks pushing their wooden boats in the pond and the girls twirling about in their pretty coats, it makes a storybook picture. Being at *Pomme* reminds me of those Parisian afternoons as the clothing here looks like it could easily be a part of a Parisian's or New Yorker's, or just about any kid's wardrobe. Couple this with beautifully crafted toys and books and décor, and the *Pomme* picture is very pretty indeed.

covet:
luco clothing
bon bon sweaters
atsuyo et akiko shirts & bags
petit pan balls
makié hats
the beatrix potter collection
tour eiffel wall sticker
jess brown design dolls

project no. 8b

the brother to project no. 8
38 orchard street. corner of hester. f: east broadway
212.925.5599 www.projectno8.com tw: @projectno8
tue - wed, sun 1 - 8p thu - sat 1 - 9p

opened in 2009. owners: brian janusiak and elizabeth beer
all major credit cards accepted

lower east side > **s46**

JH: Every time I think about *Project No. 8*, I wonder what projects numbers 1-7 were. Was project number 1 an Ebay shop selling kitten mugs? Maybe project number 2 was hand painting tea towels. Whatever the earlier projects, what matters is that Brian and Elizabeth opened *Project No. 8*, a seminal retail experience for women. Thankfully they like new projects and recently opened *Project No. 8b* a few blocks away. It has the same minimalist aesthetic, but 8b is for men. Which makes me wonder: was project number 1b selling dog mugs on Ebay?

covet:
mackintosh for project no. 8 coats
tom scott for project no. 8
chris wijnants for project no. 8
project no. 8 at the ace hotel
natalia brilli leather goods
chester wallace bags
lgr sunglasses
kostas murkudis

sacred vibes

herbal medicine apothecary

376 argyle road. corner of argyle. q: cortelyou road
718.284.2890 www.sacredvibeshealing.com
tue - sat 11a - 8p sun 11a - 5p

opened in 2009. owner: karen rose
all major credit cards accepted
online shopping. consultations. classes

ditmas park > **s47**

AB: The other day I saw a picture with before and after images of feet soaking in a full-immersion detox tub. The before picture showed normal-looking feet; the after showed cloudy blackwater, supposedly filled with the toxins pulled from the liver and gall bladder. Yikes! Am suddenly feeling the need to do a little internal cleansing. Hello, *Sacred Vibes*. Here you'll find remedies for a multitude of issues with Karen's experienced guidance. She'll help you get your insides into tip-top shape with beautiful, herbal concoctions. No need for a murky foot soup.

covet:
clear head tea
milk thistle
mugwort
marshmallow root
queen of meadow
sacred womb tea
linden flowers
lemon balm

hai Seasoning
ganic, Salt Free
Chili Powder, Coriander,

Chili Peppers Whole
Birdseye 150K HU
Organic

saipua

luscious soap and flower shop

147 van dyke. between conover and van brunt streets. bus: 61 / 77
718.624.2929 www.saipua.com tw: @saipua
sat - sun noon - 6p and by appointment

opened in 2009. owners: sarah ryhanen and eric famisan
all major credit cards accepted
custom orders / design

red hook >

CD: If my entire house looked and smelled like the tiny storefront that is *Saipua*, I would never leave. Part soap store, part floral shop, this place feels like an art installation set in an old barn. Except the "barn" is the size of a water closet and it's smack in the middle of Red Hook. *Saipua's* handmade soaps are perched amid air plants and old twine, dried lavender, antique watering cans and mason jars. A dog is curled up on a floral chair. Peonies and poppies and daffodils sprout from corners and crannies. It's easy to fall in love with *Saipua's* love of all things beautiful, innocent and pure.

covet:
soap:
  peppermint pumice
  lemon geranium
  saltwater exfoliating with nori
  rosemary mint gardeners
  mango butter
white peonies
daffodils

MANGO BUTTER SOAP $8.

FRANKINCENSE & MYRRH SOAP $8.

site

classic gift store

3511 34th avenue. between 35th and 36th. n / w: broadway > r / v: steinway
718.626.6030 www.sitedesignnyc.com tw: @sitenews
mon - sun noon - 7p

opened in 2007. owner: mackenzi farquer
all major credit cards accepted
online shopping. custom orders / design

astoria > s49

JFD: For a long time, I collected scarves and bandanas bearing the name or images of cities I'd visited. Kind of the equivalent of collecting floating landmark pens or illustrated shot glasses. Straight off, I had Paris, Vegas and LA. Easy pickings. But finding bandanas for places like Lagos, Portugal or Pendleton, Oregon, was much harder. Sometimes I've been able to track one down at that off-the-beaten path gift store. I was not surprised then, when I saw the Queens bandana at *Site*. Bingo! You'll find lots things you'll want to collect here.

covet:
dickson hairshop candles
site custom lamps
three sprouts storage bin
home stickers
tokyomilk perfume
vintage furnishings & housewares
eat local dishtowel
archie grand notebook

smith + butler

heritage clothing for men and women, oh and motorcycles

225 smith street. corner of butler. f / g: bergen street
718.855.4295 www.smithbutler.com
see website for hours

opened in 2008. owner: marylynn piotrowski
all major credit cards accepted

cobble hill > **s50**

JH: Ask any man or woman, gay or straight, to name the sexiest male movie stars of all time, and these names pop up: Paul Newman, Marlon Brando (*Streetcar* not *Apocalypse*), James Dean and Steve McQueen. These icons embodied American style. So why was there the *Flashdance* era? Or Pee-wee Herman's mini-suits? I thinks it's because we didn't have *Smith + Butler*, where old-school cool meets biker chic. Heritage brands like Pendleton and Pointer are sold alongside chic upstarts like The Hill-side. Hooray! It's okay to look brooding hot again, instead of like a malnourished whippet.

covet:
barbour
unis
belstaff
tellason
makr
iro
billy kirk
pointer brand

259

stock vintage

early american menswear

143 east 13th street. between third and fourth
l: third avenue > 4 / 5 / 6: 14th street-union square
212.505.2505
mon - fri 11a - 7p sat noon - 7p sun noon - 6p

opened in 2006. owner: melissa howard
all major credit cards accepted

east village > **s51**

JFD: When I walked into *Stock Vintage*, there was a big military duffel bag overturned, with tangled mounds of sweaters spilling out of it and greedy customers sifting through it like a bunch of 1849ers panning for gold. I guess you could say that the vintage clothing here is a kind of gold because it's harder than heck to find. Melissa scours the country to bring back dungarees and work boots and the like to this cabin-like shop. While I don't know where she mines, I imagine her digging through Nebraskan attics and Iowan closets to find this well-worn clothing that still has decades left of wear.

covet:
early american men's vintage:
  boots
  denim
  shirting
  leather jackets
  fedoras
  sweaters
  overalls

store 518

drool-worthy general store with a twist

518 court street. between nelson and huntington. f / g: smith street
646.256.5041 www.store518.com
thu - fri noon - 7p sat - sun 11a - 7p

opened in 2008. owner: nadia tarr
visa. mc
online shopping (for butter dresses only)

carroll gardens > **s52**

JH: Though this is not one of those "one-stop" shops where you can buy garden hoses and underwear simultaneously, *Store 518* does carry a little of everything: candy, antiques, curiosities, vintage and new clothing and clogs! Opening a drawer in an antique pharmacy cabinet, you might find Necco wafers in one drawer, antique hairpins in another—some items are mouth-watering and others seriously drool-worthy. And not to be missed is Nadia's signature line of jersey dresses under the Butter label. One-stop shopping, no—but a shopping must, definitely.

covet:
butter by nadia tarr
antique rulers
necco wafers
vintage clogs
the illustrated human body
winnie the pooh bike
croquet set
old wooden hangers

263

stuart & wright

dressed-down luxury clothing for women and men

85 lafayette avenue. between elliot and portland. g: fulton > c : lafayette
718.797.0011 www.stuartandwright.com tw: @stuartandwright
mon - sat noon -7p sun noon - 6p

opened in 2006. owners: alex stuart and celeste wright
all major credit cards accepted
online shopping

fort greene > **s53**

CD: I'd read that *Stuart & Wright* was the *Barney's* of Fort Greene, but I think co-owner Celeste would think that was a reach. On the other hand, the store's expertly curated mix of fashion does have a kind of *Barney's*-esque quality to it—Comme des Garçons wallets displayed in a glass case, for instance, with a little Fort Greene funk thrown in, and Rag and Bone sneakers that are just begging to hit the Brooklyn pavement. In a neighborhood that's still growing its roots, it's this type of confident, indie boutique that solidifies Fort Greene's wildcard personality.

covet:
stuart & wright sand-washed silk dresses
generic man men's shoes
mercy peacock dress
jeffrey montero scalloped women's pants
isabel marant black wool jacket
lizzie fortunato crossroad blues necklace
wendy nichol wrap leather bracelet
band of outsiders men's clothing

sweet william

indy clothing for groovy kids

112 north sixth street. between berry and wyeth. l: bedford avenue
718.218.6946 www.sweetwilliamltd.com
mon - fri 11a - 7p sat - sun noon - 7p

opened in 2007. owner: bronagh stanley
all major credit cards accepted
online shopping. registries

williamsburg > **s54**

JFD: Sweet, but with an urban edge. That's been the dressing code for the Phoebes, Sorens, Finns, Ellas, Hazels and Rubys of the last ten years. *Sweet William* hits this balance just right, with clothing and toys that are eco-conscious but not precious. Though most of my friends have settled down on the procreation front (as have I), I can imagine shopping here for the next round of kids to come, which, if my naming predictions hold, will be the Craigs and Brents, Brendas and Loris of the next decade. Naming cycles can be so cruel!

covet:
talc
nico nico clothing
ada ada
nui organics
jess brown rag dolls
atsuyo et akiko
aigle boots
hansa stuffed animals

JE T'AiME

swing: a concept shop

signature clothing, iconic furniture and so much more

1960 adam clayton powell jr boulevard. corner of 118th
2 / 3 / b / c: 116th street
212.222.5802 www.swing-nyc.com
mon, thu - sat 11a - 7p sun 10a - 6p

opened in 2009. owner: helena greene
all major credit cards accepted

harlem >

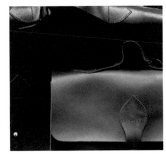

CD: I'm generally suspicious of establishments that try to do too much. How could a store selling baby clothes, furniture, jewelry, men's and women's fashion and tea really succeed? But somehow Helena manages to curate her store so seamlessly, you never once question her knack for diversification. Walking through the warm space, your eyes alight on a men's fedora, but then the smell of Kusmi tea turns your head, and then a basket of luscious silk scarves and wraps comes into view. It's a retail journey, and I enjoyed taking it.

covet:
ahene pa nkasa african bead necklace
af vandervorst black pleated skirt
ann demeulemeester georgia black silk dress
abstract mini ganesh
replica lambskin & calfsplit men's shoes
nafi de luca men's hat
bomba men's cashmere hat
album di famiglia baby shoes & mittens

269

szeki

jewelry, accessories and apparel

157 rivington street. between clinton and suffolk
f / j / m / z: essex street-delancey
646.243.1789 www.szekijewelry.com
daily 11a - 7:30p

opened in 2008. owner: szeki chen
visa. mc
online shopping

lower east side > **s56**

you can turn it into a

KW: Often when people think about this city, they think BIG. Big buildings, big restaurants and department stores, big crowds, big noise. When I think about this city, I think small. It's all about the nooks and crannies for me. And one of the sweetest little stores in town is *Szeki*. Though not much bigger than a bread box, this place and its owner of the same name, have a big heart. Here you can find not only Szeki's charmingly simple jewelry, but also wares ranging from her mom's bag line to one-off pieces she brings in from Asia. Little is good.

covet:
szekitini necklaces
szeki droppy necklaces
hamlet necklaces
little twig necklace
brass bangles
artwood bags
7115 bags & shoes
korean & japanese one-off clothing

the banquet

objects for the home and the body

360 atlantic avenue. between hoyt and bond. a / c / g / 2 / 3: hoyt-schermerhorn
718.522.6906 www.councilboutique.com
mon - fri noon - 7p sat 11a - 7p sun noon - 6p

opened in 2009. owners: pamela johnston and miranda bennett
all major credit cards accepted
custom orders

boerum hill >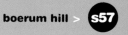

JH: Collaborations can be tricky. We need look no further than Ozzy Osbourne and Miss Piggy's rendition of "Born to be Wild" to see how egos can get in the way of success. However when a team is good, as it is at *The Banquet* (formerly *Council*), a collaboration can be greater than the sum of its parts. Here, each of the partners brings a different element of design to the table with Pamela creating the jewelry and Miranda the clothing—with both acting as curatorial voices in conjunction to the rest of the shopping story from vintage furniture and vintage clothing and curiousities. It's a harmonious convergence.

the crangi family project

some robust, some whimsical metal jewelry
9 ninth avenue. between little west 12th and 13th. a / c / e / l: 14th street
212.929.0858 www.crangifamilyproject.com
tue -sat noon - 7p sun noon - 5p

opened in 2009. owner: philip and courtney crangi
all major credit cards accepted
online shopping

**meatpacking district > **

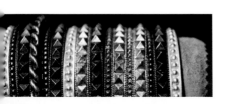

JFD: Some buy lottery tickets—I prowl the semi-annual student art sale at the Rhode Island School of Design. Someday, I figure, I'll be buying the early work of the next Chihuly or Shepard Fairey. I'm annoyed though that I didn't pick up a piece of RISD alum Philip Crangi's jewelry. This absurdly talented jeweler and his sister Courtney makes pieces that can range from delicate and sweet to steampunk and aggressive. Though I'm disappointed I didn't discover Philip early on, at least I can start collecting his pieces now at the quaint (an anomaly in the Meatpacking District) *Crangi Family Project*.

covet:
crangi line:
  mara
  forged
  venetian
gilles & brothers line:
  hook with leather lashing bracelet
pied-de-biche rings
rings & nuts necklace

tom scott

knit wonders

55 clinton street. between stanton and rivington. f / j / m / z: essex street-delancey
212.260.7591 www.tomscottnyc.com
tue - sat noon - 7p sun noon - 6p

opened in 2009. owner: tom scott
all major credit cards accepted

lower east side > **s59**

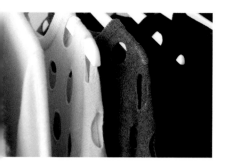

KW: Holes have an important place in fashion. Without holes, there would be no place to free important appendages from clothing. Without holes, the Sex Pistols would have been New Romantics. And without holes, *Tom Scott* would not have created his polka-dot sweater, though he is a wickedly talented guy and I suspect he would have crafted some equally clever knitted confection. A hairy shoulder piece for example. Bottom line (or hole): Tom's knits are outta this world as are his other designs, ranging from home pieces to non-knit attire.

covet:
tom scott:
  polka-dot sweater
  ra-ra skirt
  hairy loopy scarf
  draped back jump suit
  twisted back tank dress
  peek-a-boo back dress
  slashed filter tee

victor osborne

downtown milliner

160 orchard street. between stanton and rivington
f / j / m / z: essex street-delancey
212.677.6254 www.victorosborne.com
daily noon - 8p

opened in 2006. owner: victor osborne
all major credit cards accepted
online shopping. custom orders / design

lower east side >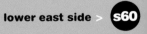

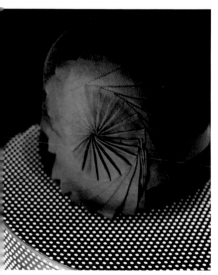

KW: Here's what makes me sad. The end of *Driving Miss Daisy*. "Your Song" by Elton John. And how flat my hair gets when I wear hats. The latter gets me the most, especially when I'm at a place like *Victor Osborne*. These aren't just some random molded felt floozies, but hand-blocked beauties each lovingly created by Victor sitting in the back of his darkly compelling atelier. As I took them all in, I was having visions of a much-needed hair transplant or maybe just a good old-fashioned perm. Actually these lids are so great, I'll just plan on never taking my chosen one off.

covet:
victor osborne:
  brigitte beret
  buckle miles
  ester
  cloche
  diamond cap
  stewardess cocktail
  trilby

VOOS

showcase for nyc based furniture and product designers

103a north third street. between berry and wyeth. l: bedford ave
718.218.8666 www.voosfurniture.com
tue - sun noon - 7p

opened in 2009. owner: serap demirag
all major credit cards accepted
custom orders / design

williamsburg > **s61**

JFD: There is a hell of a lot of creativity, mirth and clever design going on in this ever-hopping neighborhood. But even with the bar set high, *Voos* will jolt the most jaded shopper. The furniture and décor here are crafted in unusual materials and take on unexpected forms—yet surprisingly nothing feels gimmicky or forced. Each little treasure is made and produced locally by NYC designers, hence the tagline "made here, feel good." I absolutely embrace that ethos— but I personally am not going to feel good until I bring one of these pieces home.

covet:
desu design symbol coat rack
eskayel wallpapers
uhuru stoolen stools
byamt acrylic jewelry
laurie beckerman whistle lamp
takeshi miyakawa wedge table
inx design bond club chair
design glut egg pants

zero + maria cornejo

a designer's atelier

807 greenwich street. corner of jane. a / c / e / l: eighth avenue
33 bleeker street. corner of lafayette. f / b: lafayette > 6: bleeker street
212.620.0460 / 212.925.3849 www.zeromariacornejo.com
mon - sat noon - 7p sun noon - 6p

opened in 1999. owner: maria cornejo
all major credit cards accepted

greenwich village / nolita > **s62**

AB: There are a few outfits in my life that stick out in my mind. First, the Heinz ketchup Halloween outfit I wore, age 10, with my best friend who donned a matching mustard get-up. Second, my wedding dress. And third, a *Zero + Maria Cornejo* dress I borrowed from my sister. It was my first exposure to the line, and ever since, I have been an adoring fan. While taking photographs for this book, I could barely contain myself to stay on track and stick to the job at hand because all I wanted to do was drop the damn camera and try everything on. There's a lifetime of memorable clothing to be had here.

covet:
zero + maria cornejo:
  twist contra dress
  gabi trousers
  goa skirt
  loop hobo bag
  ibit dress
  shawl jacket
  bead blanket waistcoat

etc.

the *eat.shop* guides were created by kaie wellman and are published by cabazon books

eat.shop nyc 2nd edition was written, researched and photographed by kaie wellman, anna h. blessing, jan faust dane, camas davis and jon hart.

editing: kaie wellman   copy editing: lynn king   fact checking: michaela cotter santen
map and layout production: julia dickey and bryan wolf

kaie thx: the day bed with the hannah montana quilt where she watched mindless late night tv with jon and the corner bodega for providing a full array of little debbiesque packaged baked goods. she also thx the crew for keeping their chin up even after nor'easters and other squalls. camas thx jay-z for writing "empire state of mind," the ukranian mafia, melissa and brendan for their air mattress (and their love) and nicole for revealing the secret brooklyn code. jon thx brian and elizabeth and naomi. jan thx alice, henry and liz for the spectacular hospitality.

the *eat.shop* crew stayed at suite madison in the historic brooklyn neighborhood bedford-stuyvesant during production. find them at www.homeaway.com

cabazon books: *eat.shop nyc 2nd edition*
ISBN-13 9780982325469
suggested retail price: $16.95

every effort has been made to ensure the accuracy of the information in this book. however, certain details are subject to change. please remember when using the guides that hours alter seasonally and sometimes sadly, businesses close. the publisher cannot accept responsibility for any consequences arising from the use of this book.

the *eat.shop* guides are distributed by independent publishers group: www.ipgbook.com

to peer further into the world of *eat.shop* and to buy books, please visit: www.eatshopguides.com

PRINTED IN CHINA